Marrakesh
DIRECTIONS

WRITTEN AND RESEARCHED BY

Daniel Jacobs

ROUGH GUIDES

NEW YORK • LONDON • DELHI

www.roughguides.com

Contents

Introduction to

Marrakesh

Marrakesh has always had a mystique about it. A city of immense beauty – low, red and tentlike below the dramatic peaks of the High Atlas mountains – it is immediately exciting and immediately fascinating. The city is arguably the last outpost of the Mediterranean before the Sahara, yet nomadic and West African influences still seem quite distinct in the crowds and performers of the Jemaa el Fna, the main square at the heart of the old town. It's a reminder that Marrakesh was once the entrepot for goods (gold, ivory and slaves) brought by caravan across the desert.

For visitors, the Jemaa el Fna is undoubtedly the focus, a place without parallel in the world; really no more than an open space, it's also the stage for a long-established ritual in which shifting circles of onlookers gather round groups of acrobats, musicians, dancers, storytellers, comedians and fairground acts. It is always compelling, no matter how many times you return.

Almost as intriguing are the city's architectural attractions: the delicate Granada-style carving of the Saadian Tombs; the

When to visit

Weatherwise, **spring** (March–May) and **autumn** (Sept–Nov) are the best times to see Marrakesh – it'll be sunny but not too hot. At the height of **summer** (June–Aug), however, daytime temperatures regularly reach a roasting 38ºC , and don't fall below a sweaty 20ºC at night. In **winter** (Dec–Feb) the temperature may reach a pleasant 18ºC by day, but it can be grey and even wet; after dark, temperatures often drop to just 4ºC. Expect **accommodation** to be much in demand at Easter and at Christmas, when you should book well ahead.

◄ Berber dancers

magnificent rambling ruin of the El Badi Palace; the stately interior of the Bahia Palace; the exquisite Ben Youssef Medersa, a beautifully decorated Koranic school; and, above all, the Koutoubia Minaret, the most perfect Islamic monument in North Africa, whose shape and lightness of feel set the standard for all the minarets of Morocco.

Aside from these must-sees, however, the Medina, the old walled town, is the city's prime attraction; losing yourself amid this maze of irregular streets and alleys is one of the great pleasures of a visit to Marrakesh. Within its walls you'll find a profusion of mosques, Koranic schools and *zaouias* (tombs of holy men and women), amid what is, for most Western

▲ Medina spice stall

visitors, an exotic street life, replete with itinerant knife-grinders and fruit sellers, mules bearing heavy goods through the narrow thoroughfares, and country people in town to sell wares spread out upon the ground. It's also within the

▲ Tea, Moroccan style

Medina that you'll find the city's main museums: the Marrakesh Museum, housed in a beautiful nineteenth-century palace; Dar Si Said, with its amazing collection of woodwork artefacts; and the Maison Tiskiwin, with exhibits on the trans-Saharan connection between Marrakesh and Timbuktu.

In the Medina's many traditional workplaces, artisans such as blacksmiths, weavers, hatters, tanners and carpenters still ply ancient trades. Many of their wares end up in the Medina's souks, where you can spend hours wandering labyrinthine passages in search of souvenirs and haggling for handicrafts over endless cups of mint tea. Marrakesh's modern shops may lack the quaint charm of the souks, but they're worth perusing for low-priced leatherware, household accessories and fine *objets d'art*.

For dining, as much as for shopping, Marrakesh is a city of new experiences. You can feast on classic Moroccan dishes like pastilla (sweet poultry pie) and tanjia (jugged beef or lamb) in the palatial splendour of an eighteenth-century Medina mansion, or enjoy delicious tajine (Moroccan casserole) or couscous at any of the Jemaa el Fna's night-time food stalls. The city also has its share of fine French and Italian restaurants, and boasts a surprisingly exuberant nightlife.

When you need a break from the bustle of the city streets, you'll find

▲ Essaouira ramparts

beautiful, historic and surprisingly extensive gardens all around the city, and – within a couple of hours' striking distance – the peaks and valleys of the High Atlas, where wild flowers dot pastoral landscapes beneath the rugged wildness of sheer rock and snow. Also not far away, on the coast, is the friendly, picturesque walled town of Essaouira. It's a centre for fine art as much as water sports, not to mention some excellent seafood dining.

>> MARRAKESH AT A GLANCE

▲ The Jemaa El Fna

The Jemaa el Fna

All of Moroccan life is here in this magical square – traditional performers, fortune-tellers, hawkers and ordinary Moroccans seduced by the unique vibe.

The Northern Medina

The section of the walled city north of the Jemaa el Fna is home to Marrakesh's souks and most of the artisans' workshops, plus some notable Islamic monuments.

▶ Souk Smarine

▲ El Badi Palace

The Southern Medina

Less crowded than the Northern Medina, the area south of the Jemaa el Fna features the city's royal palaces, the lavish Saadian Tombs and a couple of worthwhile museums.

The Ville Nouvelle

Founded by the French when they took over in 1912, the new city outside the Medina walls is the centre of Marrakesh's nightlife and café culture, and the location of its poshest restaurants and chic boutiques.

The gardens and the palmery

Marrakesh is surrounded by green, with a trio of classic gardens: the huge, walled Agdal, the Menara with its olive and citrus groves, and the exquisitely designed Majorelle. Northeast of town is the palmery, a rambling oasis of date trees.

◄ Ville Nouvelle architecture

◄ Menara gardens

Ideas

Top six sights

As a visitor to Marrakesh, you won't find any shortage of things to see and do – almost every nook and cranny of the Medina has something of interest, and even shopping and eating out can provide a whole new experience. Among the sights, the **must-sees** include two impressive palaces (one in ruins, the other restored), the most ornate burial site in North Africa, a beautifully designed 1920s garden, and the most amazing city square in the whole world.

Koutoubia Mosque

The classic Moroccan minaret, simply perfect in its proportions and its decoration.

▸ P.53 ▸ JEMAA EL FNA AND THE KOUTOUBIA ▲

Bahia Palace

The ideal of Arabic domestic architecture expressed in a classic nineteenth-century palace.

▸ P.65 ▸ THE SOUTHERN MEDINA AND AGDAL GARDENS ▲

El Badi Palace

The "Incomparable Palace", now an incomparable ruin.

▶ P.61 ▶ THE SOUTHERN MEDINA AND AGDAL GARDENS ▲

Saadian Tombs

The most exquisitely decorated mausoleum in North Africa, encrusted in fine tilework and dripping with carved stucco.

▶ P.64 ▶ THE SOUTHERN MEDINA AND AGDAL GARDENS ▲

The Jemaa el Fna

The city square that's an open-air circus, starring snake charmers, acrobats, storytellers and musicians.

▶ P.51 ▶ JEMAA EL FNA AND THE KOUTOUBIA ▲

Majorelle Garden

A brilliant designer garden, with cacti, lily ponds and a stunning, cobalt blue Art Deco pavilion.

▶ P.86 ▶ THE VILLE NOUVELLE ▼

Houses of Prayer

Religion has always dominated life here, and the **mosque** lies at the very heart of the community. As well as the *jemaa*, a mosque designed for communal Friday prayers, there is the *masjid*, an everyday neighbourhood mosque, and the *zaouia*, the tomb of a holy person, whose blessing is believed to touch those who pray within. Attached to many mosques is a *medersa*, or religious school; *medersas* were at one time the only source of formal education. The city also has its synagogues, catering for a Jewish community no less religious than their Muslim neighbours.

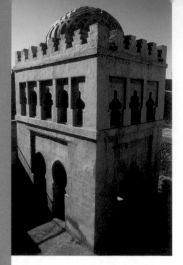

Almoravid Koubba

This small domed structure is the only piece of Almoravid-era architecture left standing in Morocco, and was probably used for performing ablutions before prayer.

▶ P.75 ▶ THE NORTHERN MEDINA ▲

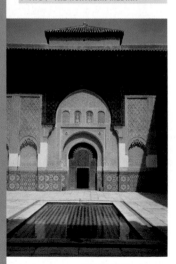

Ben Youssef Medersa

Carved wood, stucco and tilework – no surface is left undecorated in this ancient former Koranic school.

▶ P.76 ▶ THE NORTHERN MEDINA ▲

Lazama Synagogue

This kabbalistic chart, in the Jewish quarter's most important synagogue, underlines the importance of mysticism in local religion.

▸ P.66 ▸ **THE SOUTHERN MEDINA AND AGDAL GARDENS** ▸

Zaouia of Sidi Ben Salah

Featuring a fourteenth-century minaret, the *zaouia* is the focal point of spiritual life in the surrounding quarter.

▸ P.79 ▸ **THE NORTHERN MEDINA** ▲

Zaouia of Sidi Bel Abbes

The tomb of Marrakesh's most important holy man, patron saint of the city's blind.

▸ P.80 ▸ **THE NORTHERN MEDINA** ▸

Squares

As you wander the dense forest of buildings and alleyways that make up the Medina, chancing upon a square is like arriving in a clearing, open to the sky, where you can stop and catch your breath. As often as not each square was an ancient marketplace, and some squares retain that function today, while others have become gardens.

Rahba Kedima

Apothecary stalls dominate this space at the heart of the Medina souks.

▶ P.74 ▶ THE NORTHERN MEDINA ▲

Criée Berbère

Once slaves were sold here – today it's the scene of a carpet and *jellaba* auction.

▶ P.74 ▶ THE NORTHERN MEDINA ▲

Place des Ferblantiers

The tinsmith's square – now partly a rose garden – where craftsmen construct beautiful lanterns in tin, brass and glass.

▶ P.61 ▶ THE SOUTHERN MEDINA AND AGDAL GARDENS ▲

The Grand Mechouar

By the Royal Palace, this immaculate space is one of three squares, called *mechouars*, which originally served as palace courts, where petitioners to the sultan would await admission.

▶ P.67 ▶ THE SOUTHERN MEDINA AND AGDAL GARDENS ▼

Place de la Kissaria

Emerge from the souks into this square surrounded by major sights, with the Almoravid Koubba, the Marrakesh Museum and the Ben Youssef Medersa adjoining each other.

▶ PP.75–76 ▶ THE NORTHERN MEDINA ▶

Museums and galleries

Marrakesh's **museums** are arguably of interest more for the buildings that house them than for the exhibits they contain, but you'll certainly want to look around inside if you have a special interest in woodcarving or in Moroccan and Islamic arts. Lately a new wave of modern artists have created a stir in Marrakesh, and a handful of exciting **art galleries** have sprung up to exhibit their work, both in the Medina and in the Ville Nouvelle.

Islamic Arts Museum

Yves Saint Laurent's personal collection of North African carpets, ceramics and furniture, housed in a brilliant cobalt-blue house amid cacti and lily ponds.

▶ P.88 ▶ THE VILLE NOUVELLE ▲

Marrakesh Museum

This imposing nineteenth-century politician's mansion now houses exhibitions of Moroccan art and sculpture.

▶ P.76 ▶ THE NORTHERN MEDINA ▲

Maison Tiskiwin

A unique collection of Moroccan and Malian artefacts illustrating the trans-Saharan caravan trade with Timbuktu, on which Marrakesh's economy was once based.

▶ P.60 ▶ THE SOUTHERN MEDINA AND AGDAL GARDENS ▼

Dar Si Said

A beautiful old mansion with a great collection of carved cedarwood, some of it adorning the building itself, not to mention some wonderful stuccowork.

▶ P.60 ▶ THE SOUTHERN MEDINA AND AGDAL GARDENS ▲

La Galerie Bleu

The Ville Nouvelle's newest modern art gallery, exhibiting the work of Morocco's leading artists.

▶ P.89 ▶ THE VILLE NOUVELLE ▼

Indulgent Marrakesh

There are plenty of sensual **pleasures** to explore in Marrakesh, often for very little money. A steam bath at a hammam comes complete, if you want it, with a **massage** and rub-down; for something even more relaxing, try a massage with aromatic oils. Alternatively, have a henna tattoo or order sumptuous pastries at one of the city's patisseries. For those who can afford it, the city's **luxury hotels** offer gourmet food, opulent furnishings and staff at your beck and call day and night.

Pastries and confections

To indulge your sweet tooth, Marrakesh boasts not only French-style patisseries serving fine cream cakes, but also traditional stalls in the souks offering syrup-soaked delicacies.

▶ P.83 ▶ THE NORTHERN MEDINA ▲

Hotel Mamounia

Stay at what Winston Churchill called "the most beautiful place in the world", all massive chandeliers and Art Deco touches, and set in extensive grounds.

▶ P.111 ▶ ACCOMMODATION ▲

The hammam

Men and women have separate entrances to the Turkish-style steam bath, where the principle is to sweat it all out and rub all the dirt off. You'll emerge glowing.

▶ P.126 ▶
ESSENTIALS ▶

Aromatic body massage

The totally relaxed feeling that comes from having sweet oils massaged into your skin is only enhanced by a cup of mint tea or herbal infusion afterwards.

▶ P.69 ▶ THE SOUTHERN MEDINA ▼

Henna tattoos

Have a design painted on your hands, as Moroccan women do for their wedding. It should not wash off for at least three weeks.

▶ P.52 ▶ THE JEMAA EL FNA AND
THE KOUTOUBIA ▲

La Maison Arabe

The most de luxe hotel in town boasts palatial splendour, immaculately kept patios, superb food, even its own cookery school.

▶ P.113 ▶ ACCOMMODATION ▼

The city gates

Marrakesh's **ramparts**, 15km in circumference and 2m thick, are punctuated by nineteen city gates. Many of these are modern, though the walls themselves, made of pisé (clay and straw), mostly date back to the city's foundation under the Almoravids in the eleventh century. Some of the gates are clearly defensive but others were designed to impress visitors entering. The more recent gates are much simpler – sometimes just breaches in the wall – and were added to improve access to the Medina.

Bab Debbagh

The "tanner's gate" gives access to a quarter of the Medina suffused with the smell of leather being soaked in urine.

▸ P.79 ▸ THE NORTHERN MEDINA ▴

Bab Agnaou

This nineteenth-century gate was the city's main entrance for common people.

▸ P.65 ▸ THE SOUTHERN MEDINA AND AGDAL GARDENS ▴

Bab Taghzout

Close to one of the city's important *zaouias*, this striking ochre gateway was part of the city walls until they were extended beyond it in the eighteenth century.

▶ P.80 ▶ THE NORTHERN MEDINA ▶

Bab el Khemis

The "Thursday Gate" was named for the Thursday market held outside – though these days there's a market every day.

▶ P.80 ▶ THE NORTHERN MEDINA ▼

Bab Ighli

An impressive double-arched gate leading to the Royal Palace and the Agdal gardens.

▶ P.67 ▶ THE SOUTHERN MEDINA AND AGDAL GARDENS ▲

The Jemaa el Fna

Without the Jemaa el Fna, said novelist Paul Bowles, Marrakesh would be just another Moroccan city, and certainly this square is the city's **heart and soul**. Here you'll find acrobats and storytellers, snake charmers and tooth-pullers. In the evening you can sit down to a full meal while a motley crew of itinerant musicians play long into the night.

Tooth-pullers

Their methods may look crude and brutal, but these practitioners offer the only toothache treatment most Moroccans can afford.

▶ P.51 ▶ THE JEMAA EL FNA AND THE KOUTOUBIA ▲

Medicine men

Remedies, spells and potions, aphrodisiacs even, of origins animal, vegetable and mineral – and not a pill or a capsule in sight.

▶ P.51 ▶ THE JEMAA EL FNA AND THE KOUTOUBIA ▲

Acrobats

Marrakesh's acrobats are surprisingly adroit – so much so that many have gone on to delight audiences in European circuses.

▶ P.53 ▶ THE JEMAA EL FNA AND THE KOUTOUBIA ▶

Jemaa dining

Everything from spaghetti to sheeps' heads is on offer at the evening food stalls, where you can dine in an atmosphere unmatched by any restaurant.

▶ P.58 ▶ THE JEMAA EL FNA AND THE KOUTOUBIA ◀

Khendenjal

A spicy drink served with an equally spicy nut-based confection. The drink is supposedly an aphrodisiac – if you're with the right person, try it and see.

▶ P.58 ▶ THE JEMAA EL FNA AND THE KOUTOUBIA ▶

Fortune-tellers

In Marrakesh you can have your cards read by wise women under umbrellas, or get a talisman made up, as often as not using Koranic verses, though such practices aren't endorsed by orthodox Islam.

▶ P.52 ▶ THE JEMAA EL FNA AND THE KOUTOUBIA ◀

Dead Marrakesh

This is a city that respects its dead. Muslims are never cremated after death, but are **buried** with their heads towards Mecca. Elaborate gravestones are not the custom, though somebody particularly holy may have a domed tomb – a *koubba* – erected over their grave. Some two hundred such holy men and women, known as **marabouts**, are buried in Marrakesh; the tombs of the seven most prominent (the "seven saints") have formed a circuit for pilgrims since the seventeenth century.

Tomb of Sidi Abdel Aziz

This *zaouia* is among the smallest of the tombs of the city's seven saints.

▶ P.77 ▶ THE NORTHERN MEDINA ▲

Tomb of Sidi Ali Belkacem

Some *koubbas* stand alone, but many, like this one, can be found amid the graves of an ordinary Muslim cemetery.

▶ P.54 ▶ THE JEMAA EL FNA AND THE KOUTOUBIA ▲

Tomb of Fatima Zohra

A whitewashed shrine in the shadow of the Koutoubia, and commemorating one of Marrakesh's few female saints.

▶ P.54 ▶ THE JEMAA EL FNA AND THE KOUTOUBIA ▶

Saadian Tombs

The mausoleum for a whole dynasty of sultans, from the great Ahmed el Mansour to the mad Moulay Yazid.

▶ P.64 ▶ THE SOUTHERN MEDINA AND AGDAL GARDENS ▼

Miâara Jewish cemetery

Hump-like graves standing in neat rows as far as the eye can see characterize this seventeenth-century plot, serving Marrakesh's once sizeable Jewish community.

▶ P.66 ▶ THE SOUTHERN MEDINA AND AGDAL GARDENS ▼

Cafés

When **coffee** first arrived in the Islamic world, many Muslim jurists argued that it should be banned as it was an intoxicant. More moderate voices prevailed, and the café became an important feature of life in many Muslim countries. In Morocco its position was reinforced by the French colonials, who added their own style of café society. Today the cafés perform the role that bars have traditionally had in many Western countries, largely a male preserve, a place to hang out with friends or watch football on TV. But they're also the place for a morning croissant, or a pot of mint tea come the afternoon.

Café-Restaurant El Badi

A handy place for a coffee, or even a meal, if you're visiting the nearby El Badi palace, whose walls – complete with nesting storks – you can see from the terrace.

▶ P.69 ▶ THE SOUTHERN MEDINA AND AGDAL GARDENS ▲

Café Le Siroua

A small, friendly café with excellent coffee, handy for breakfast and open long hours.

▶ P.91 ▶ THE VILLE NOUVELLE ▲

Café-Restaurant Argana

Pop up for a pot of tea and enjoy one of the best views over the Jemaa el Fna.

▶ P.58 ▶ THE JEMAA EL FNA AND THE KOUTOUBIA ▲

Solaris

Quite a glitzy pavement café, where you can relax in wicker chairs and have a leisurely read of your newspaper over a coffee and croissant.

▶ P.92 ▶ THE VILLE NOUVELLE ▼

Boule de Neige

There's a range of fine coffees, breakfasts and ice creams here, not to mention the ambrosial honey, almond and argan paste known as *amalou*.

▶ P.91 ▶ THE VILLE NOUVELLE ▲

Café-Restaurant Toubkal

Here's a place that does tasty *msammen* – something between a French crepe and an Indian *paratha*, served with honey for breakfast.

▶ P.56 ▶ THE JEMAA EL FNA AND THE KOUTOUBIA ▼

Marrakesh after dark

In a town where good girls don't stay out late, the **nightlife** is rather staid, but it's there if you want it. Most of the upmarket hotels have bars where a woman can at least enjoy a drink without the presumption that she must be on the game, and nightclubs where you can shake your booty to a variety of sounds. In the Medina, the Jemaa el Fna offers a very different sort of after-dark experience – open-air dining amid a veritable circus of street performers.

Diamant Noir nightclub

North African *raï* sounds are the dance-floor filler at this popular downtown club.

▶ P.95 ▶ THE VILLE NOUVELLE ▲

VIP

Enjoyable, if slightly sleazy, two-level club with folk music upstairs and disco sounds below.

▶ P.95 ▶ THE VILLE NOUVELLE ▲

The Jemaa el Fna by night

Dine under the stars to the accompaniment of rhythmic Gnaoua music from the square's wandering musicians.

▶ P.51 ▶ THE JEMAA EL FNA AND THE KOUTOUBIA ▲

Paradise Disco

Marrakesh's poshest disco is only partially successful at being exclusive, but it's a good night out all the same.

▶ P.95 ▶ THE VILLE NOUVELLE ▲

Hotel Mamounia Casino

Topnotch jacket-and-tie casino, which promises to stay open "until you run out of money".

▶ P.71 ▶ THE SOUTHERN MEDINA AND AGDAL GARDENS ◀

Chesterfield Pub

Not as English as it would like to be, this "pub" is nonetheless one of Casablanca's more atmospheric watering holes.

▶ P.94 ▶ THE VILLE NOUVELLE ▶

Green Marrakesh

Especially in summer, when temperatures rise to the high thirties Celsius (the high nineties in Fahrenheit), the middle of the day is sometimes best devoted to inactivity, and where better for that than the city's **gardens**. Two of them – the Agdal and Menara – were designed for that purpose. Each begins near the edge of the Medina, rambles through acres of orchards and olive groves and has, near its centre, an immense pool, once thought to cool the air. Much smaller and more tended and landscaped is the gorgeous Jardin Majorelle.

The palmery

Date palms and suburban villas make the Marrakesh's own oasis a sought-after residential location, as well as a pleasant retreat from the city bustle.

▶ P.96 ▶ OUTSIDE THE CITY

Majorelle Garden

Twentieth-century French painter Jacques Majorelle's beautifully landscaped garden has an impressive collection of cacti.

▶ P.86 ▶ THE VILLE NOUVELLE

Bab Jedid olive grove

Olives are one of Morocco's agricultural mainstays – even in Marrakesh it's easy to find them growing, in a grove that's also a popular picnic spot.

▶ P.88 ▶ THE VILLE NOUVELLE ▼

The Agdal gardens

Watered by ancient underground channels, the gardens were founded with the city itself and provided a picnic spot for the sultan and his entourage.

▶ P.67 ▶ THE SOUTHERN MEDINA AND AGDAL GARDENS ▲

The Menara gardens

Tranquil by day, the pool and pavilion here are the setting for a night-time "Marvels and Reflections" show of dance and acrobatics.

▶ P.88 ▶ THE VILLE NOUVELLE ▶

Souvenirs

There are plenty of wonderful souvenirs to buy in Marrakesh – among them rugs and carpets, pottery and ceramics, silver jewellery, inlaid wood (marquetry) and leather. Whatever you buy, and wherever you buy it, you're expected to **bargain**. There are no hard and fast rules to bargaining – it is really about paying what something is worth to you. Don't think that you need to pay a specific fraction of the first asking price: some sellers start near their lowest price, while others will make a deal for as little as a tenth of the initial price.

Jewellery

Arabic gold jewellery is usually a little too gaudy for Western tastes, but some of the silver pieces – including silver bangles and chunky rings – can be very attractive.

▶ P.54 ▶ THE JEMAA EL FNA AND THE KOUTOUBIA ▲

Thuya marquetry

Some lovely items are made from the wood and root of the thuya tree, often inlaid with other woods.

▶ P.81 ▶ THE NORTHERN MEDINA ▲

Tyre crafts

Used car and bicycle tyres are turned into kitsch but appealing picture frames and mirror frames, as well as more practical buckets and baskets.

▶ P.68 ▶ THE SOUTHERN MEDINA AND AGDAL GARDENS ▶

Ceramics

Fine pottery from the kilns at Salé and Safi on the coast is on sale at most of Marrakesh's souvenir outlets, even in the municipal market.

▶ P.90 ▶ THE VILLE NOUVELLE ◀

Teapots

The perfect vessel for making "le whisky maroccain" (as mint tea is jokingly known) – though the right sort of mint might be hard to find once you're home.

▶ P.54 ▶ THE JEMAA EL FNA AND THE KOUTOUBIA ▶

Musical instruments

Lutes, whether classic, wooden *ouds* or rustic, skin-covered *ginbris*, as well as drums made of wood or glazed earthenware, make good souvenirs and fine instruments if you can play them.

▶ P.69 ▶ THE SOUTHERN MEDINA AND AGDAL GARDENS ◀

Clothing and headgear

You probably wouldn't want to walk down the streets of Liverpool or Los Angeles wearing a traditional Moroccan **robe**, but you might want to lounge around at home in one. Moroccan **slippers** are a favourite buy – exotic, stylish and comfortable. For women, accessories such as **scarfs** are worth considering, as are the dresses on sale at the city's boutiques.

Babouches

Moroccan slippers, traditionally yellow, but available in plenty of other colours too.

▶ P81 ▶ THE NORTHERN MEDINA ▲

Fezzes

Look like a character from the Ottoman Empire in the traditional tasselled red hat that originated in Marrakesh's long-time rival city of Fes.

▶ P.73 ▶ THE NORTHERN MEDINA ▲

Dresses

Traditional dresses don't try to flatter the figure, though if you want a slinky little number you can head for Marrakesh's new boutiques.

▸ P.83 ▸ THE NORTHERN MEDINA ▼

Jellabas

Popular with hippy visitors in the 1960s, the *jellaba* is ordinary streetwear here, but works better as a nightgown in the West.

▸ P.83 ▸ THE NORTHERN MEDINA ▶

Knitted caps

Brightly coloured skullcaps – you'll need short hair to wear them – are a big favourite with Moroccan men.

▸ P.73 ▸ THE NORTHERN MEDINA ▲

Scarfs

The *kissaria*, at the heart of the souk area, is the place to find silk and cotton scarfs in any colour you could imagine.

▸ P.83 ▸ THE NORTHERN MEDINA ◀

Artisans at work

Marrakesh is alive with **cottage industries**, worked by skilled artisans using methods that have barely changed over the centuries, and continuing trades that have all but died out in the West. On a wander through the Medina you'll find tanneries and smithies, weavers at their looms, hatters making hats and shoemakers making shoes. In fact these workshops are in many ways much more interesting – though no larger than – the shops selling the goods they produce, and the artisans may be able to sell you items you see being finished.

Blacksmiths

Railings, window grilles or furniture – no metal creation is too complex for local blacksmiths and ironmongers.

▶ P.75 ▶ THE NORTHERN MEDINA ▲

Dyers

The dyers have the Medina's most colourful souk, hung with hanks of wool in all the colours of the rainbow.

▶ P.75 ▶ THE NORTHERN MEDINA ▲

Tanners

Pigeon droppings are one of the substances
used to tan leather in this rather dirty job.

▸ P.79 ▸ THE NORTHERN MEDINA ▼

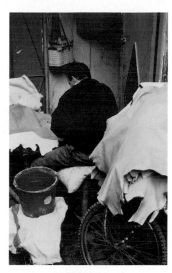

Leatherworkers

Fresh from the city's tanneries, leather is
made into all manner of consumer durables.

▸ P.75 ▸ THE NORTHERN MEDINA ▲

Carpet weaver

Handlooms are still used to produce
Moroccan carpets, each a one-off piece.

▸ P.82 ▸ THE NORTHERN MEDINA ▼

Sports and activities

Within easy reach of Marrakesh are the High Atlas mountains, perfect for a **hike** or, from December to April, **skiing**. Just a little further away, coastal Essaouira is a popular centre for **windsurfing**. Closer at hand there are three eighteen-hole **golf** courses just outside Marrakesh itself. For something more sedentary, let yourself be transported around town in a horse-drawn carriage, or get along to one of Marrakesh's cinemas, which offer quite a contrast to the flicks at home.

Windsurfing

Reliable winds at Essaouira ensure some of the best windsurfing in North Africa.

▶ P.103 ▶ ESSAOUIRA ▲

Atlas trekking

Crystalline mountain air, snowy peaks and green valleys await trekkers and hikers in the High Atlas.

▶ P.97 ▶ OUTSIDE THE CITY ▲

Skiing at Oukaïmeden

Just two hours from Marrakesh you'll find 20km of runs for skiers and snowboarders at all levels.

▶ P.98 ▶ OUTSIDE THE CITY   ▲

Golf

Morocco's late king, Hassan II, enjoyed a spot of golf, and the country has some top-class courses, including three excellent ones around Marrakesh.

▶ P.126 ▶ OUTSIDE THE CITY   ▶

Calèche rides

Sit back in a horse-drawn carriage and ride around town or through the palmery in style.

▶ P.120 ▶ ESSENTIALS   ▲

Going to the cinema

The standard double bill of Bollywood epic and Hong Kong chop-sockie is seldom as interesting as sharing a theatre with Marrakshi youths shouting, whistling, cheering and jeering right through the show.

▶ P.125 ▶ ESSENTIALS   ▶

Marrakesh motifs

The features and motifs of Moroccan architecture are pretty much standard, but each theme has produced myriad variations. Islam's suspicion of representational art – making an image of a person or an animal is considered but a short step from idolatry – has given rise to a penchant for **geometrical designs**. In Marrakesh's **palaces** you'll find rich stuccowork, painted wooden ceilings and stained-glass windows. **Religious buildings** are especially likely to be decorated with *zellij* (mosaic tilework), particularly around the *mihrab* (niche indicating the direction of Mecca), and motifs like *darj w ktarf* (cheek and shoulder) or *shabka* (net) on the minaret.

Darj w ktarf

This fleur de lys-like pattern, here used above the windows at the top of the Koutoubia, has been a favourite in Moroccan architecture since the time of the Almohads.

▸ P.53 ▸ THE JEMAA EL FNA AND THE KOUTOUBIA ▲

Stucco

Some of the most intricate designs are carved into plaster on lintels, cornices and walls, notably at the Saadian Tombs.

▸ P.64 ▸ THE SOUTHERN MEDINA AND AGDAL GARDENS ▲

Castellations

The battlements atop so many of Marrakesh's gates and palaces are decorative as much as defensive.

▶ P.80 ▶ THE NORTHERN MEDINA ▲

Zellij

Every building with *zellij* tilework actually uses its own motif, based on a star with a specific number of points – sixteen in this example from the Saadian Tombs.

▶ P.64 ▶ THE SOUTHERN MEDINA AND AGDAL GARDENS ▼

Carved cedarwood

Especially in the form of panels and lintels, cedarwood with inscriptions and stylistic designs carved into it surmounts walls, doorways and recessed fountains. This example is in the Ben Youssef Medersa.

▶ P.77 ▶ THE NORTHERN MEDINA ▼

Painted wooden ceilings

The cedarwood ceilings of Marrakesh's mansions and palaces are adorned with beautiful hand-painted traditional designs; some of the best can be seen at the Bahia Palace.

▶ P65 ▶ THE SOUTHERN MEDINA AND AGDAL GARDENS ▲

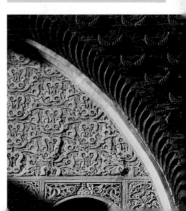

Dining

With some sumptuous dining to be had in Marrakesh, gourmets won't go hungry. The mainstay of Moroccan cuisine is the **tajine**, a casserole traditionally cooked on its own charcoal stove called a *kanoun*. Some of the best places to eat are **palace restaurants**, housed in beautifully restored old mansions (though choose carefully: the worst of these are real tourist traps, with mediocre food and inflated prices). Most restaurants offer a set menu of starter, main course and dessert, sometimes with tea and coffee thrown in and, at grander establishments, additional courses.

Rotisserie de la Paix

Excellent grill restaurant where you can dine alfresco in summer or by a cosy fire in winter.

▶ P.94 ▶ THE VILLE NOUVELLE ▲

Couscous

Berber in origin, this is the classic north African dish: steamed semolina pellets, moist and aromatic. It's served with meat, fish or vegetables – classically seven vegetables in fact. Try it at *Le Tobsil*.

▶ P.57 ▶ THE JEMAA EL FNA AND THE KOUTOUBIA ▲

Palais Gharnatta

Enjoy a belly-dancing spectacle while feasting on the usual Moroccan classics at this opulent restaurant.

▶ P.70 ▶ THE SOUTHERN MEDINA AND AGDAL GARDENS ▲

Snall stew

You pull the molluscs – bought from vendors in the Jemaa el Fna – out of their shells with a toothpick, then drink the soup.

▶ P.58 ▶ THE JEMAA EL FNA AND THE KOUTOUBIA ▲

La Taverne

Marrakesh's oldest restaurant still serves good Moroccan and French food at reasonable prices.

▶ P.92 ▶ THE VILLE NOUVELLE ▼

Tajine

The classic tajines are chicken with olive and preserved lemon, and lamb with prunes and almonds.

▶ P.56 ▶ THE JEMAA EL FNA AND THE KOUTOUBIA ▲

Festivals and events

Marrakesh and its hinterland aren't short of annual events of all descriptions. Among the religious festivities are **moussems**, local affairs commemorating particular holy men or women. There are also sporting events and cultural festivals, notably a celebration of popular – here meaning traditional – arts.

Moussem at Setti Fatma

In August you can combine a hike in the Ourika Valley with the annual shindig at its main village.

▶ P.97 ▶ OUTSIDE THE CITY ▲

The Marrakesh Marathon

In January athletes from Morocco and abroad come to run this gruelling but scenic race around the Medina and through the palmery.

▶ P.124 ▶ ESSENTIALS ▲

The Marrakesh Film Festival

Catherine Deneuve is among the glitterati who've flocked to Marrakesh for this prestigious cinematic event, held in October.

▶ P.124 ▶ ESSENTIALS ▼

The Marrakesh Festival

An equestrian "fantasia" is held outside the city walls every evening during Marrakesh's week-long festival of popular arts, held in June.

▶ P.124 ▶ ESSENTIALS ▼

Ramadan

Practising Muslims fast from dawn to sunset in the holy month of Ramadan, the fast broken each evening with a meal that traditionally features soup, dates and eggs.

▶ P.123 ▶ ESSENTIALS ▲

Places

Places

The Jemaa el Fna and the Koutoubia

Once upon a time, every Moroccan city had a main square where storytellers and musicians entertained the townspeople. Even then, the Jemaa el Fna drew the greatest variety of performers, and the best. Today, it's the only one left. By day there are just a few entertainers, but in the evening it becomes a whole carnival; come here and you'll soon be squatting amid the onlookers and contributing a dirham or two. For a respite, the café and restaurant rooftop terraces here afford a view over the square and of the Koutoubia minaret – as much a symbol of Marrakesh as Big Ben is of London.

Jemaa el Fna

The Jemaa el Fna is recognized by UNESCO as a "masterpiece of the oral and intangible heritage of humanity". Nobody is entirely sure when or how the square came into being – or even what its name means. The usual translation is "assembly of the dead", which could refer to the public display here of the heads of rebels and criminals, since the Jemaa was a place of execution well into the nineteenth century. An alternative translation is "mosque of nothing", which would refer to an abandoned sixteenth-century plan for a new great mosque on the site.

By day, activity in the square is sparse: a handful of **snake charmers** bewitch their cobras with their flutes, **medicine men** (especially in the northeast of the square) display cures and nostrums, while **tooth-pullers** wielding fearsome pliers offer to pluck the pain from out of the heads of toothache sufferers, trays of

extracted molars attesting to their skill. It isn't until late afternoon that the square really gets going, as storytellers, acrobats and musicians appear

▼ WATER SELLERS

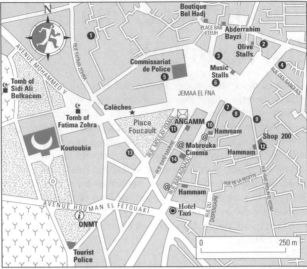

▼ QESSABIN MOSQUE, NORTHEAST OF THE SQUARE

(see box opposite). There are sideshow attractions too: games of hoop-the-bottle, **fortune-tellers** sitting under umbrellas with packs of fortune-telling cards at the ready, and women with piping bags full of **henna** paste, ready to paint "tattoos" on hands, feet or arms that will last up to three months (though beware of black – as opposed to natural red – henna, as this contains a toxic chemical).

For **refreshment**, stalls offer freshly squeezed orange and grapefruit juice, while neighbouring handcarts are piled high with dates, dried figs and almonds and walnuts, especially delicious in winter when they are freshly picked in the surrounding countryside. And as dusk falls, the square

Performers in the Jemaa el Fna

The tourists' favourite among the square's performers are the **snake charmers**, always photogenic (though you have to pay them for the privilege of a snapshot). Moroccans, however, prefer the **storytellers**, great raconteurs who draw quite a throng – it's around them that you'll see the biggest circles gathered. Also in attendance are acrobats (the square has for years supplied European circuses), child boxers, sad-looking trained monkeys, clowns and Berber boy dancers – whose routines, to the climactic jarring of cymbals, are totally sexual, and traditionally an invitation to clients.

Dozens of **musicians** in the square play all kinds of instruments. In the evening there are full groups: members of the **Aissaoua**, one of Morocco's biggest Sufi brotherhoods, playing oboe-like *ghaitahs*; **Gnaoua** trance-healers, members of a Sufi brotherhood of Senegalese origin, who beat out hour-long hypnotic rhythms with clanging iron castanets and pound tall drums with long curved sticks; and groups playing the classical Arabic music of **Andalusia** in southern Spain, from where their forebears were expelled back in the sixteenth century. Late into the night, when almost everyone has gone home, you'll still find players plucking away at their lute-like *ginbris*.

becomes a huge **open-air dining area**, packed with stalls lit by gas lanterns, the air filled with plumes of cooking smoke spiralling up into the night (see box on p.58 for more).

The Koutoubia

Rising dramatically from the palm trees to the west of the square, the Koutoubia minaret – nearly seventy metres high and visible for miles on a clear morning – is the oldest of the three great towers built by Morocco's eleventh-century Almohad rulers (the others are the Hassan Tower in Rabat and the Giralda in Seville).

Work on the minaret probably began shortly after the Almohad conquest of the city, around 1150, and was completed under Sultan Yacoub el Mansour (ruled 1184–99).

The Koutoubia's **proportions** – a 1:5 ratio of width to height – give it an extraordinary lightness of feel and became the standard for minarets throughout Morocco. Indeed the Koutoubia displays many features that were to become widespread in Moroccan architecture – the wide band of **ceramic inlay** near the top, the **castellated battlements** rising above it, the **darj w ktarf** ("cheek and shoulder" – similar to the French *fleur de lys*) and other motifs – and the alternation of patterning on the different faces. At the summit are three great copper balls, thought to have been made of gold originally, and possibly a gift from Yacoub el Mansour's wife, presented as penance for breaking her fast for three hours during Ramadan.

Originally the minaret was covered with plaster and painted. To see just how much this can change the whole effect – and, to most tastes, lessen much of its beauty – take a look at the Kasbah mosque (also known as the Mosque el Mansour, located by the Saadian Tombs; see p.64) which has been restored in this manner. It was decided not to do that when the Koutoubia was restored at the end of the 1990s, though the work did include new floodlighting – seen to stunning effect in the evening, when the minaret and the neighbouring gardens are something of a focus for promenading Marrakshis.

The tombs of Fatima Zohra and Sidi Belkacem

The white *koubba* (domed mausoleum) alongside the Koutoubia is the **tomb of Fatima Zohra**, the daughter of a seventeenth-century religious leader. Tradition has it that she was a woman by day and a white dove by night, and women still dedicate their children to her in the belief that her blessing will protect them. Another marabout's shrine, the **tomb of Sidi Ali Belkacem**, stands just to the northwest of the Koutoubia. Like many saints' tombs, it lies within an ordinary cemetery (which only Muslims may enter); you can get glimpse of it through the cemetery gate.

Shops

Abderrahim Bayzi

160 Place Bab Fteuh ☎044 42 91 57. Daily 8am–8pm. Teapots and tea glasses are what you'll find here, lots of them, for serving up mint tea. There are aluminium pots for decoration only, and stainless steel ones that you can actually use, all in the typically Moroccan "pointed pear" shape, plus glasses both plain and fancy. To check prices before you start to haggle, pop round the corner to one of the hardware shops behind the Commissariat de Police in the north of the Jemaa el Fna, where you'll find similar items at fixed prices.

Boutique Bel Hadj

22 & 33 Souk Fondouk Louarzazi, Place Bab Fteuh ☎044 44 12 58. Daily 9.30am–7pm. If silver is your thing, this is the place to look, with heavy silver bracelets from around Morocco and as far afield as Afghanistan, sold by weight and purity. There's other

▾RUE RIAD ZITOUN EL KEDIM, OFF THE JEMAA EL FNA

▲ OLIVE STALL

silverware too – antique teapots for example (and often as not made for the Moroccan market in the exotic English city of Manchester), along with tea trays.

Music stalls

At the eastern end of the foodstalls area in the Jemaa el Fna, opposite Souk Jedid. Daily 10am–midnight.
Three stalls offering a good selection of Moroccan and Arabic cassettes (usually 15–20dh) and CDs (80–100dh). Most are of Algerian *raï* and Egyptian pop – the music that dominates Moroccan radio – but the stalls also have homegrown *raï* and *chaabi* (folk music), and if you ask they'll play you Berber music from the Atlas, classical Andalusian pieces from Muslim-era Spain, music from Marrakesh's great rival city of Fes, even hypnotic Gnaoua music.

Olive stalls

Souk Ableuh. Daily 10am–8pm.
Located in a little square just off the Jemaa el Fna is this row of stalls with olives piled up at the front. The wrinkled black ones are the most typical Moroccan olive, delicious with bread but a bit salty on their own. As for the green olives, the ones flavoured with bits of lemon are among the tastiest. Also on sale here are the spicy red harissa sauce and bright yellow lemons preserved in brine, the brine taking the edge off the lemons' acidity; they're a favourite ingredient in Moroccan cooking. A jar of them also looks great on a kitchen shelf.

Shop 200

200 Rue Riad Zitoun el Kedim. Daily 8.30am–1pm & 3–9.30pm. Handy little outlet (unsigned, so look for the number "200") with a better range of postcards than available on the square, and at slightly lower prices. Also stocks a good selection of maps.

Cafés and patisseries

Café du Grand Balcon

South side of the square, next door to the Hotel CTM. Daily 9am–10pm.
Though not quite as close to

▲ ENTRANCE TO THE CTM HOTEL

the action as the *Restaurant Argana* (see p.58), this place has the fullest view over the Jemaa, taking it all in from the perfect vantage point. In the evening the best tables get taken quickly, though at other times you should have no trouble getting a table with a view. However, it serves no food, only tea, coffee and sodas.

Hotel CTM
South side of the square. Daily 7am–11pm. In addition to offering a view onto most of the square, the hotel's rooftop café does a very good-value Continental breakfast (7–11am; 20dh), but otherwise only serves drinks.

Patisserie des Princes
32 Rue Bab Agnaou. Daily 5am–midnight. A sparkling patisserie with mouth-watering pastries at prices that are a little high by local standards, but well worth the extra. They also have treats like almond milk and ice cream. The *salon de thé* at the back is a very civilized place to take breakfast, morning coffee or afternoon tea.

Restaurants and food stalls

Café-Restaurant Toubkal
Southeast corner of Jemaa el Fna, by Rue Riad Zitoun el Kedim. Daily 5am–midnight. As well as fruit juices, home-made yoghurts and pastries, they offer a range of salads, tajines and couscous. This is also a great place for a breakfast of coffee plus bread and jam or *msammen* (a paratha-like griddle bread) with honey. You'll be hard-put to spend more than 50dh.

Chez Bahia
50m down Rue Riad Zitoun el Kedim. Daily 6am–midnight. A café-diner offering pastilla, wonderful tajines (bubbling away at the front) and low-priced snacks, plus breakfasts of *bisara*, which is a thick pea soup with olive oil and cumin, and freshly made *harsha*, a delicious dense griddle bread with a gritty crust. You can eat well here for 50dh.

Hotel Ali
Rue Moulay Ismail. Daily 6.30–10pm. This popular hotel serves a great-value buffet supper every

▲ BUFFET, HOTEL ALI

evening, on the roof in summer, inside during the winter. The spread features *harira*, salads, couscous and ten or more tajine-style dishes, including several vegetable ones, plus Arabic pastries and fruit for dessert. Eat as much as you like for 60dh (50dh for hotel residents).

Hotel de Foucault

Av el Mouahidine, facing Place de Foucault. Daily 7–11pm. Set menus at the hotel restaurant cost 80–200dh, but the place is most notable for its suppertime all-you-can-eat buffet – a huge choice of fine dishes including

pastilla and various meat and vegetable tajines. At 120dh, it's twice the price of the buffet at the *Hotel Ali*, but more than twice as good.

Le Tobsil

22 Derb Abdellah Ben Hessaien ℡044 44 40 52. Daily except Tues 7–11pm. Sumptuous Moroccan cuisine in an intimate riad, reached by heading south down a little alley just east of Bab Laksour. This is considered by many to be the finest restaurant in town, with delicious pastilla and the most aromatic couscous you could imagine, though the wine (included in the price) doesn't match the quality of the food. Worth booking ahead; the set menu – which changes daily – is 550dh.

Restaurant Al Baraka

1 Place Jemaa el Fna, by the Commissariat de Police ℡044 44 23 41. Daily 11.30am–2pm and 8pm–midnight. A stylish Moroccan restaurant in a beautiful garden and with a tastefully decorated interior. The food is terrific, from the range of salads (including carrot perfumed with orange blossom water) to the beautifully tender chicken and lamb tajines. In the evenings

▼ JUICE STALLS

they lay on music and belly-dancing (not really Moroccan, but what the hell). Set menus 300–400dh.

Café Restaurant Argana

North side of the square. Daily 5am–midnight. The Jemaa's closest vantage point and not at all a bad place to eat. Dishes include lamb tajine with prunes and a seafood pastilla, a new-fangled version of the traditional poultry pie. Set menus are 90–130dh.

Restaurant du Progrés

20 Rue Bani Marine. Daily noon–midnight. One of the best budget restaurants in town, with friendly service, excellent-value set menus, huge steaming portions of couscous, and change out of 50dh.

Restaurant Marrakechi

52 Rue des Banques ☎ 044 44 33 77. Daily noon–6pm & 7pm–midnight. High up above the square, the *Marrakechi* has imperial but intimate decor, impeccable service and superb food,

including an indescribably delicious pastilla. There are three set menus: the cheaper ones (220dh or 250dh) feature a choice of six tajines or five different couscous dishes, each including a vegetarian option, or there's a 310dh menu which allows you to have a tajine *and* a couscous dish, if you can fit it all in.

Tanjia stalls

Souk Ableuh; daily noon–10pm. One of the most quintessential Marrakshi dishes is tanjia (also spelt tangia or tanzhiya), beef – or sometimes mutton – cooked very slowly in an urn of that name. Most good restaurants in town offer tanjia, and there are cheap tanjia joints serving nothing else – almost every Medina district has such a place, identifiable by the urns at the front. The most convenient of these are the trio of outlets in Souk Ableuh (opposite the olive stalls) which seem to take it in turns to open.

If you drop by in advance you can have your tanjia cooked to

Jemaa food stalls

Marrakesh's tourist guides often suggest that the Jemaa's food stalls (open daily from dusk until 11pm) aren't very hygienic, but, as the cooking is so visible, standards of cleanliness are probably higher than in many kitchens. As well as couscous and pastilla, there are spicy **merguez** sausages, salads, fried fish, and – for the more adventurous – **sheep's heads** complete with eyes.

To partake, just take a seat on one of the benches and order all you like. If you want a soft drink or mineral water with your meal, the stallholders will send a boy to get it for you. Note that stalls which don't clearly display their prices are likely to overcharge you mercilessly, so make sure to ask the price before ordering.

Besides sit-down meals, you'll find exotic snacks on offer too. Over towards the eastern side of the square, a group of stalls offer a food much loved in Morocco – stewed **snails**. The stallholder ladles servings out of a simmering vat, and you eat the snails with a pin or toothpick before slurping back the soup they are stewed in. Just south of the main food stalls are a row of vendors selling **khendenjal**, a hot, spicy infusion based on ginseng and said to be an aphrodisiac. It's usually accompanied by a spicy confection made of flour and ground nuts, and served by the spoonful.

▲ AN EVENING STROLL THROUGH THE SQUARE

order. The meat and seasonings (garlic, cumin, nutmeg and other spices) will then be placed in the urn for you and taken to the man who stokes the furnace at the local hammam. When the urn emerges from the embers after a few hours, the meat is tender and ready to eat.

The Southern Medina and Agdal gardens

The biggest attractions in the southern half of the Medina are the fabulous ruin of the **El Badi Palace** and the exquisite **Saadian Tombs**. Both lie within the **Kasbah** district, which was originally Marrakesh's walled citadel. To the east of here is the **Royal Palace**, used by the king when visiting the city (and not open to the public). The area east of this is the **Mellah**, once Morocco's largest Jewish ghetto; the extensive **Agdal gardens** lie to the south. Between the Royal Palace and the Jemaa el Fna, the residential **Riad Zitoun el Kedim** and **Riad Zitoun el Jedid** quarters are home to two interesting museums and the beautiful **Bahia Palace**.

Dar Si Said

Riad Zitoun el Jedid. Daily except Tues 9am–12.15pm & 3–6.15 pm. 20dh. A smaller version of the Bahia Palace, Dar Si Said was built in the late nineteenth century for

▾MINARET OF THE KASBAH MOSQUE

the brother of Bou Ahmed (see p.65) who, like Bou Ahmed himself, became royal chamberlain. It's a pleasing building, with beautiful pooled courtyards, scented with lemons, palms and flowers, and it houses an impressive **Museum of Moroccan Arts**. The museum is particularly strong on its collection of eighteenth- and nineteenth-century woodwork, most of it in cedar. Besides the furniture, there are Berber doors and window frames, all hand-carved in beautifully irregular shapes, and wonderful painted ceilings. There are also (upstairs) a number of traditional wedding **palanquins**, once widely used for carrying the bride, veiled and hidden, to her new home.

On the way out, don't miss the seats from a rustic fairground-style contraption like a small wooden Ferris wheel, on which children commonly rode at *moussems* until the early 1960s. Photographs illustrate the apparatus as it was when in use.

▲ PLACE DES FERBLANTIERS

Maison Tiskiwin

Riad Zitoun el Jedid. Daily (though not reliably) 10am–12.30pm & 3–6pm. 15dh. The Maison Tiskiwin houses a unique collection of Moroccan and Saharan artefacts, billed as "a journey from Marrakesh to Timkbuktu and back". Furnished from the collection of Dutch anthropologist Bert Flint, the exhibition underlines the longstanding cultural links across the desert, a result of the centuries of **caravan trade** between Morocco and Mali. Each of the rooms features carpets, fabrics, clothes and jewellery from a different region of the Sahara, with explanatory notes in French.

Place des Ferblantiers

This tinsmiths' square, formerly called Place du Mellah, was once part of the old Jewish souk. The southern part of the square is now surrounded by the workshops of **lantern makers**, while the northern half has become quite a pretty little rose garden.

El Badi Palace

Bab Berrima. Daily 8.30–11.45am & 2.30–5.45pm. 10dh. Sultan Ahmed el Mansour's sixteenth-century El Badi Palace is substantially in ruins, reduced throughout to its red *pisé* walls, but enough remains to suggest that its name – **"The Incomparable"** – was not entirely immodest. What you see today is essentially the ceremonial part of the complex, planned on a grand scale for the reception of ambassadors.

The original entrance was in the southeast corner, but today you enter from the north, through the **Green Pavilion**, emerging into a vast **central courtyard** over 130m long and nearly as wide. In the northeast corner, you can climb up to get an overview from the ramparts, and a closer view of the **storks** nesting atop them.

Within the central courtyard are four sunken gardens, each pair separated by a pool, with smaller pools in the four corners of the courtyard. When filled – as during the June folklore festival (see

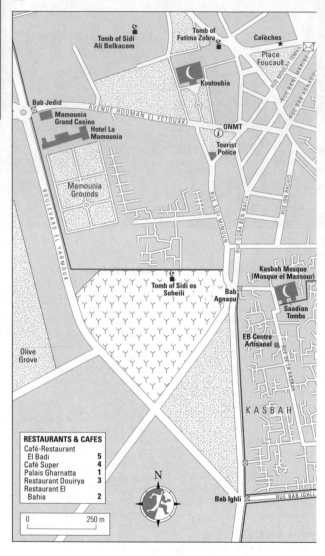

Map labels:
- Tomb of Sidi Ali Belkacem
- Tomb of Fatima Zohra
- Calèches
- Place Foucauld
- RUE MOULAY ISMAIL
- RUE BAB AGNAOU
- RUE BANI MARINE
- Koutoubia
- Bab Jedid
- AVENUE HOUMAN EL FETOUAKI
- ONMT
- Mamounia Grand Casino
- Hotel La Mamounia
- Tourist Police
- RUE SIDI MIMOUN
- RUE OQBA BEN NAFIA
- RUE IBN RACHID
- Mamounia Grounds
- BOULEVARD EL YARMOUK
- Kasbah Mosque (Mosque el Mansour)
- Tomb of Sidi es Soheili
- Bab Agnaou
- Saadian Tombs
- EB Centre Artisanal
- RUE DE LA KASBAH
- Olive Grove
- KASBAH
- Bab Ighli
- RUE BAB IGHLI
- N

RESTAURANTS & CAFES

Café-Restaurant El Badi	5
Café Super	4
Palais Gharnatta	1
Restaurant Douirya	3
Restaurant El Bahia	2

0   250 m

p.124) – they are an incredibly majestic sight.

You can pay another 10dh to see the original **minbar** (pulpit) from the Koutoubia mosque (see p.53), housed in a pavilion in the southwest corner of the main courtyard. Once one of the most celebrated works of art in the Muslim world, it was commissioned from the Andalusian capital Cordoba in 1137 and took eight years to complete. The whole structure

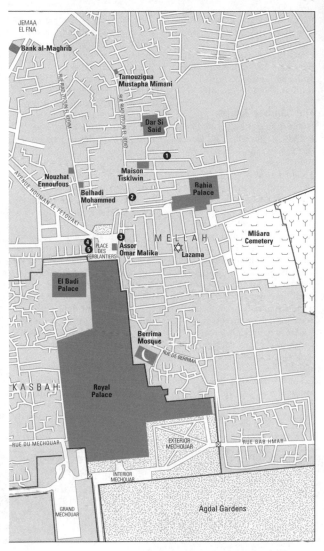

was covered with the most exquisite inlay work of which, sadly, only patches remain. The minbar was removed from the Koutoubia in 1962 for restoration, and eventually brought here.

South of the courtyard are the ruins of the **palace stables** and, beyond them, leading towards the walls of the present royal palace, a series of **dungeons**, used into the last century as a state prison. You can explore part of these and could easily spend an hour or two wandering the various courtyards above, with their fragments of marble and *zellij*, and water conduits for the fountains and hammams.

The Saadian Tombs

Rue de la Kasbah. Daily 8.30–11.45am & 2.30–5.45pm. 10dh. The tombs of the Saadians – the dynasty which ruled Morocco from 1554 to 1669 – escaped plundering by the rapacious Sultan Moulay Ismail, of the subsequent Alaouite dynasty, probably because he feared bad luck if he desecrated them. Instead, he blocked all access bar an obscure entrance from the Kasbah mosque. The tombs lay half-ruined and half-forgotten until they were rediscovered by a French aerial survey in 1917. Restored, they are today the Kasbah's main sight – over-lavish in their exhaustive decoration, but dazzling nonetheless.

The finer of the two **mausoleums** in the enclosure is on the left as you come in – a beautiful group of three rooms.

Architecturally, the most important feature here is the **mihrab** (the niche indicating the direction of Mecca), its pointed horseshoe arch supported by an incredibly delicate arrangement of columns. The room itself was originally an oratory, probably not intended for burial use, though now almost littered with the narrow marble tombstones of Saadian princes. Also buried here is the "mad sultan" **Moulay Yazid**, whose 22-month reign was one of the most sadistic in the nation's history.

Opposite the *mihrab*, an elaborate arch leads to the domed central chamber and the tomb of Sultan Ahmed el Mansour, flanked by those of his sons and successors. The room is spectacular, faint light filtering onto the tombs from an interior lantern in a tremendous vaulted roof, the *zellij* full of colour and motion.

It was Ahmed who built the other mausoleum, older and less impressive, above the tombs of his mother and of the Saadian dynasty's founder, Mohammed

▼ TILEWORK AND CARVED STUCCO, THE SAADIAN TOMBS

esh Sheikh. The latter is buried in the inner room – or at least his torso is, since the Turkish mercenaries who murdered him took his head back to Istanbul for public display.

Outside, round the garden and courtyard, are scattered the tombs of over a hundred more Saadian princes and members of the royal household. Like the privileged 66 given space within the mausoleums, their gravestones are brilliantly tiled and often elaborately inscribed.

Bab Agnaou

One of the two original entrances to the Kasbah, this magnificent blue granite gateway was built in 1885. The name actually means "black people's gate", a reference to the gate's use by swarthy commoners, while the fair-complexioned aristocracy had their own gateway (now long gone). The entrance is surrounded by concentric arches of decoration and topped with an inscription in decorative script, which reads: "Enter with blessing, serene people."

The Bahia Palace

Rue Riad Zitoun el Jedid. Daily 9am–3pm. 10dh. The Bahia Palace – its name means "brilliance" – was originally built in 1866–7 for the then grand vizier (akin to a prime minister), **Si Moussa**. In the 1890s it was extended by his son, **Bou Ahmed**, himself a grand vizier

▲ CITY WALLS, NEAR BAB AGNAOU

and regent to the sultan, who ascended the throne aged 14. There is a certain pathos to the empty, echoing chambers of the palace, and the inevitable passing of Bou Ahmed's influence and glory. When he died, the palace was looted by its staff, and his family driven out to starvation and ruin.

You enter the palace from the west, through an arcaded courtyard. This leads through to a small riad (enclosed garden), part of Bou Ahmed's extension and decorated with beautiful carved stucco and cedarwood surrounds. The adjoining eastern salon leads through to the **great courtyard** of Si Moussa's palace, with a fountain in its centre and vestibules on all sides, each boasting a marvellous painted wooden ceiling.

South of the great courtyard is the large riad, the heart of Si

Moussa's palace, fragrant with fruit trees and melodious with birdsong, approaching the very ideal of beauty in Arabic domestic architecture. The halls to the east and west are decorated with fine *zellij* fireplaces and painted wooden ceilings. From here, you leave the palace via the private apartment built in 1898 for Ahmed's wife, **Lalla Zinab**, where again it's worth looking up to check out the painted ceiling, carved stucco and stained-glass windows.

The Mellah

Set up in 1558, Marrakesh's **Jewish ghetto** was almost a town in itself in the sixteenth century, presided over by rabbis, with its own souks, gardens, fountains and synagogues. Jewish ghettos in Morocco were called *mellah* ("salter"), supposedly because residents of the first – in Fes – had the job of salting the decapitated heads of executed criminals for display on the city walls.

Jewish quarters often adjoined the sultan's palace, a situation which could provide a useful diversion in times of unrest, when protestors could vent their anger on the Jews rather than the sultan. But the main reason for gathering the Jews in one quarter was to make it easier to tax them. Though most of its members were poor, the Jewish community also included practically all of the city's bankers, metalworkers, jewellers and tailors.

The present-day Mellah, however, is almost entirely **Muslim** – most of the Jews left long ago for Casablanca, France or Israel. The quarter is immediately distinct, with taller houses and narrower streets than elsewhere in the Medina. Would-be guides may offer (for a tip, of course) to show you some of the surviving synagogues, notably the **Lazama** (open to the public daily 7–9am & 6–8pm except Friday evenings, all day Saturdays and Jewish holidays; there's no charge, but a tip is expected).

The **Miâara Jewish cemetery** on the east side of the Mellah is reckoned to date from the early seventeenth century. Among the tombs are eleven shrines to Jewish

▼ MIÂARA JEWISH CEMETERY

marabouts (*tzadikim*), illustrating an interesting parallel between the Moroccan varieties of Judaism and Islam. The cemetery can be visited any day except Saturdays and Jewish holidays.

Bab Ighli and the Mechouars

Immediately south of the Kasbah, **Bab Ighli** is a relatively recent gateway, which nonetheless manages to look quite splendid. The gate is one route to the three **Mechouars** (the other is to head south from the Saadian tombs, along Rue de la Kasbah and then Rue du Mechouar). These were walled enclosures where the Sultan's troops used to parade, and where petitioners to the throne would await an audience; nowadays they're largely taken up by flower gardens.

Agdal gardens

Fri & Sun 8am–5.30pm. Free. Over the centuries the Agdal gardens (access via the path leading south from the Interior Mechouar; bus #6 from Place Foucault will take you to the path's southern end) have been tended, abandoned and revived on a number of occasions. That said, the layout – a confusingly large expanse, some 3km in extent, dating from the nineteenth century – probably differs little from its predecessors. The gardens are surrounded by walls, with gates (closed) at each of the northern corners. Once you're out of sight of the walls, it feels as if you're in the countryside rather

▲ CHICKPEAS SOLD ON THE STREET

than in a city garden. Inside, the orange, fig, lemon, apricot and pomegranate **orchards** are divided into square plots by endless raised walkways and broad avenues of olive trees. The area is watered by an incredible system of wells and **underground channels**, known as *khettera*, that go as far as the base of the Atlas and date, in part, from the very founding of the city.

At the heart of the gardens lies a series of pools, the largest of which is the **Sahraj el Hana** (the Tank of Health – now a green, algae-clogged rectangle of water). Probably dug during Almohad times, it's flanked by a ramshackle old **summer pavilion**, where the last few precolonial sultans held picnics and boating parties. You can climb up on its roof for a fabulous view over the park and across to the Koutoubia and the Atlas.

La Mamounia hotel and gardens

Av Bab Jedid. It's worth popping into Marrakesh's top hotel for a pot of tea on the terrace and a look at the opulent interior, with its 1920s Art Deco touches. The terrace overlooks the hotel's **gardens**, which regular visitor Winston Churchill described to his friend Franklin D. Roosevelt – when they were here together in 1943 – as the loveliest spot in the world. Walled off from the outside bustle, yet only a few minutes' walk from the Jemaa el Fna, the gardens were once royal grounds, laid out by the Saadians with a succession of pavilions. Today they're somewhat Europeanized in style but have retained the traditional elements of citrus trees and walkways. Note that visitors are

not supposed to enter the hotel wearing shorts or jeans.

Shops

Assor Omar Malika

35 Place des Ferblantiers ☎062 60 63 02. Daily 8am–8pm. A big selection of brass and iron lanterns in all shapes and sizes, doubling up as light shades for boring old electric bulbs. The many-pointed star-shaped lanterns with glass panes are a big favourite, as are simple candle-holder lanterns, but there are larger and grander designs too.

Belhadi Mohammed

144 Rue Riad Zitoun el Kedim. Daily 8am–10pm. This is one of a group of small shops at this end of the road which recycle disused car tyres. Initially they made hammam supplies such as buckets and flip-flops, but they've since branched out into products such as picture frames and framed mirrors, odd rather than elegant in black rubber, but certainly worth a look. The square bicycle-tyre picture frames are the most appealing buys here, but the

▼ TYRE CRAFTS

▲ STORKS ON THE EL BADI PALACE WALLS

round mirror frames designed to look like stylized suns have a certain kitsch charm.

EB Centre Artisanal/ Maison du Tapis

7 Derb Baissi Kasbah, Rue de la Kasbah ☎044 38 18 53. Daily 8.30am–8pm. A massive craftwork department store with a huge range of goods at fixed prices, only slightly higher than what you might pay in the souks. The sales assistants who follow you round are generally quite charming and informative. Carpets (around 2000dh for a decent-sized example) are the best buy, but there's a huge selection of clothing, ceramics, brassware and even furniture.

Nouzhat Ennoufous

61 Rue Riad Zitoun el Kedim ☎044 42 80 81. Daily 10.30am–10pm. Although it bills itself as a *salon de thé* (tea room), this is actually a massage parlour where you can have your worldly woes rubbed away using aromatic oils (rose, apricot, lavender, rosemary or the uniquely Moroccan sweet argan oil), with a relaxing cup of tea or a herbal infusion to conclude. You'll emerge relaxed,

unwound, fragrant and glowing. A one-hour whole-body massage with five oils is 250dh.

Tamouzigua Mustapha Mimani

84 Kennaria Teoula, off Rue Riad Zitoun el Jedid. Daily 9am–8pm. This small shop specializes in Moroccan musical instruments, most notably drums, which they make themselves in their neighbouring workshop (they also offer lessons in how to play them). Also on sale are the lute-like *ginbris*, which make excellent souvenirs to hang on your wall back home.

Cafés

Café-Restaurant El Badi

Off Place des Ferblantiers by Bab Berrima. Daily 9am–9.30pm. On a rooftop looking out over Place des Ferblantiers and towards the Mellah, this is one place to get close to the storks nesting on the walls of the El Badi Palace. It serves a limited range of hot and soft drinks, and a modest 80dh set menu of soup, salad and couscous, with a Moroccan sweetmeat for afters.

Café Super

Place des Ferblantiers. Daily
7am–9.30pm. The tea and coffee
are decent enough, but there's
nothing really special about this
common-or-garden male-
dominated Moroccan café –
except that it's a great place to
watch televised football with the
locals. Any big Champions'
League matches will certainly
be on the box, attracting avid
attention from the clientele.
Women, however, may feel
conspicuous here, especially
inside.

Restaurants

Palais Gharnatta

5–6 Derb el Arsa, off Rue Riad Zitoun
El Jedid ☎044 38 96 15,
🌐www.gharnata.com. Daily from 8pm
(book before 5pm). Popular with
foreign visitors, though
unfortunately the food (pastilla,
couscous, lamb tajine) is merely
so-so, and individual diners play
second-fiddle to groups.
However the decor is splendid,
as the building is a
magnificently decorated
sixteenth-century mansion,
with an Italian alabaster
fountain at its centre; scenes
from *The Return of the Pink
Panther* were shot here. Past
patrons have included
Jacqueline Kennedy and the
Aga Khan.

Restaurant Douirya

14 Derb Jedid, near Place des
Ferblantiers ☎044 38 38 36,
🌐www.restaurantdouirya.com. Daily
noon–3pm & 8pm–midnight. *Douirya*
means "small house", but this is in
fact a palatial establishment
with a remarkable painted
wooden ceiling. Open for lunch
(250dh) and dinner (350dh for a
menu of pastilla followed by
tanjia; 420dh featuring pigeon
stuffed with honey and
almonds), when there's also
music and belly dancing. Easy to
find, in the southeast corner of a

▾ GRAND ENTRANCE TO THE RESTAURANT EL BAHIA

square by the Place des Ferblantiers.

Restaurant El Bahia

1 Rue Riad Zitoun El Jedid, by the Bahia Palace ☏044 37 86 79. Daily 7pm–midnight. A beautifully restored palatial mansion offering set menus based on specialities of Marrakesh (beef and prune tajine, couscous *aux sept legumes* or *chakchouka*; 350dh) or Fes (pastilla or chicken tajine with olive and preserved lemon; 380dh). There's music and dancing to keep you entertained while you eat.

Casino

Grand Casino

Hotel La Mamounia, Av Houman el Fetouaki. Mon–Fri 5pm–4am, Sat & Sun 3pm–4am (gaming tables from 9pm). Walking in from the Medina, you'll find this grand, high-class casino pretty unreal. Under huge chandeliers and Art Deco glass panels, you can – so long as you're not Muslim – gamble your life savings on roulette, craps or blackjack, or feed your change to the slot machines. Entrance is free, but scruffy clothes aren't permitted; men need a jacket and tie.

The Northern Medina

Great for souvenir shopping, the main area of **souks**, or markets, is centred on a main thoroughfare, **Souk Smarine**. Once each souk was clearly defined, with one street selling this, another selling that, but nowadays the souks also feature a variety of shops catering primarily to tourists. Among the most interesting souks are the **Rahba Kedima**, with its apothecary stalls, and the **dyers' souk**, hung with brightly coloured hanks of freshly dyed wool. North of the souks are the small but architecturally important **Almoravid Koubba**, the

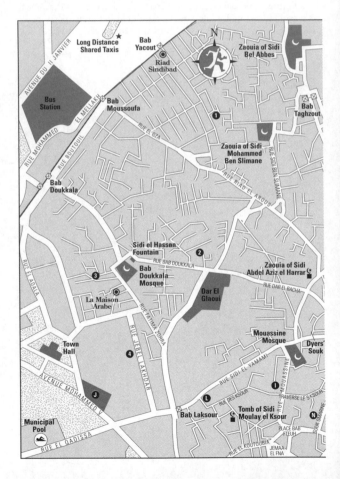

Marrakesh Museum and the beautifully decorated **Ben Youssef Medersa**. Beyond, in all directions, are the ordinary residential quarters of the Medina.

Souk Smarine

Busy and crowded, Souk Smarine is an important thoroughfare, covered along its whole course by an **iron trellis** that restricts the sun to shafts of light dappling everything beneath, especially in the early afternoon. Historically the street was dominated by the sale of textiles and clothing. Today, classier tourist "bazaars" are moving in, with American Express signs in the windows, but there are still dozens of shops in the arcades selling and tailoring traditional shirts and kaftans. Other shops specialize in multicoloured cotton skullcaps and in **fezzes**, whose

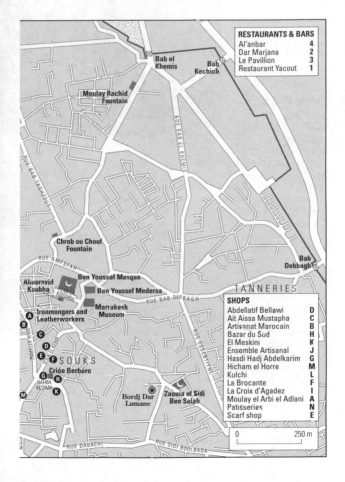

RESTAURANTS & BARS

Al'anbar	4
Dar Marjana	2
Le Pavillion	3
Restaurant Yacout	1

SHOPS

Abdellatif Bellawi	D
Ait Aissa Mustapha	C
Artisanat Marocain	B
Bazar du Sud	H
El Meskini	K
Ensemble Artisanal	J
Hasdi Hadj Abdelkarim	G
Hicham el Horre	M
Kulchi	L
La Brocante	F
La Croix d'Agadez	I
Moulay el Arbi el Adlani	A
Patisseries	N
Scarf shop	E

0   250 m

Map labels: Bab el Khemis, Bab Kechich, Moulay Rachid Fountain, RUE BAB EL KHEMIS, RUE BAB TAGHZOUT, Chrob ou Chouf Fountain, RUE AMESFAH, Bab Debbagh, Almoravid Koubba, Ben Youssef Mosque, Ben Youssef Medersa, RUE BAB DEBBAGH, TANNERIES, RUE EL KEDIMA, Ironmongers and Leatherworkers, Marrakesh Museum, SOUK ATTARIN, SOUKS, Criée Berbère, RAHBA KEDIMA, Bordj Dar Lamane, Zaouia of Sidi Ben Salah, RUE ESSEBTYNE, RUE DABACHI, RUE SIDI BOULBADA

proper name *tarbouche fassi* derives from the city of Fes in northern Morocco, where they originate. The feeling of being in a labyrinth of hidden treasures is heightened by the passages among the shops, leading through to small covered markets. The occasional stucco-covered doorways between shops are entrances to mosques, havens of spiritual refreshment amid the bustle.

Rahba Kedima

Souk Smarine narrows just before the fork at its northern end. The passageways to the right (east) here give a glimpse of the Rahba Kedima, a small ramshackle square with a few vegetable stalls set up in the middle of it.

Immediately to the right as you go in is **Souk Btana**, where whole sheepskin pelts are displayed and laid out to dry on the roof. Most interesting, however, are the **apothecary stalls** in the southwest corner of the square, selling **traditional cosmetics** – earthenware saucers of cochineal (*kashiniah*) for lip-rouge, powdered *kohl* eyeliner (traditionally antimony trisulphide, but nowadays more commonly lead sulphide – both are toxic), henna (the only cosmetic unmarried women are supposed to use) and sticks of *suek* (walnut root or bark) for cleaning teeth. The stalls also sell

▲ SOUK SMARINE

herbal and animal ingredients still in widespread use for protection against – or the making of – magic spells, with roots and tablets for aphrodisiacs, dried pieces of lizard and stork, fragments of beaks and talons, even gazelle horns.

La Criée Berbère

Until the French occupied the city in 1912, La Criée Berbère ("the Berber auction") was the site of **slave auctions**, held just before sunset every Wednesday, Thursday and Friday. Most of the slaves had been kidnapped and marched here with the camel caravans from Guinea and Sudan – those too weak to make it were left to die en route.

Only rugs and carpets are sold here nowadays, and there's usually a small auction around

4pm. The latter is an interesting sight, with the auctioneers wandering round the square shouting out the latest bids, but it's not the best place to buy a rug – it's devoted mainly to heavy, brown woollen **jellabas**.

Kissaria

A covered market at the heart of the souk area, the Kissaria was originally set up as the market for rich imported **fabrics**. It remains the centre for cloth and clothing, offering an array of beautiful dresses, flowing headscarfs and roll upon roll of fine material.

Souk Sabbaghine

The Souk Sabbaghine (or Souk des Teinturiers, the **dyers' souk**), is west of the Kissaria and very near the sixteenth-century Mouassine Mosque and fountain. On a good day, it has a splendid array of freshly dyed sheaves of wool in a multitude of colours hung out to dry. At other times you'll barely see any at all, though you can still take a look as the dyers boil up their tints and prepare the wool for treatment. The natural dyes of

yore have largely given way to brighter synthetic colours, and the gutters are often awash with rivulets of different hues vying for dominance.

Souk Haddadine and Souk Cherratine

It's easy to locate Souk Haddadine, the **ironmongers' souk**, by ear – just head towards the source of the bangings and clangings as the artisans shape raw metal into decorative window grilles, lampstands and furniture. Close at hand you'll find Souk Cherratine, the **leatherworkers' souk**, full of workshops where hats, slippers and other goods are cut and stitched by hand, plus specialist shops whose sole occupation is to grind and sharpen tools.

The Almoravid Koubba

On the south side of Place de la Kissaria. Daily 9am–1pm & 2.30–6pm. 10dh. Situated well below today's ground level, the Almoravid Koubba (correctly called the Koubba Ba'adiyn) doesn't look like much, but this small, two-storey structure is the only building in Morocco to survive

▼ STREET ICE-CREAM VENDOR

intact from the eleventh-century Almoravid dynasty, whose style lies at the root of all Moroccan architecture. The windows on each side exhibit the classic shapes of Moroccan design – as do the merlons (the Christmas-tree-like battlements), the complex "ribs" on the outside of the dome, and the dome's interior support, a sophisticated device of a square and star-shaped octagon, which is itself repeated at each of its corners. Among the remains of the attendant facilities are a large water cistern and latrines and fountains for performing ablutions, much like those adjoining many Moroccan mosques today. Indeed the Almoravid Koubba was probably an ablutions annexe to the **Ben Youssef Mosque** opposite, which, like almost all the Almoravids' buildings, was demolished and rebuilt by the succeeding Almohad dynasty.

The Marrakesh Museum

Place de la Kissaria. Daily 9.30am–6pm. 30dh. This building was once a magnificent late-nineteenth-century palace built for defence minister Mehdi Mnebb, later Morocco's ambassador in London. Neglected for many years, it was restored and opened in 1997 as a museum to house exhibitions of Moroccan **art and sculpture**, both traditional (in the main hall and surrounding rooms), and contemporary (in what were the palace kitchens). It is the building itself, however, that is most memorable, especially the warren of rooms that was once the **hammam**, and the now-covered **inner courtyard** with its huge brass lamp hung above above a central fountain. There's also a small café and bookshop in the entrance courtyard.

The Ben Youssef Medersa

Off Place de la Kissaria. Daily 9am–6pm. 20dh. Just north of the Marrakesh Museum is the Ben Youssef Medersa, a **religious school** where students learned the Koran by rote. Attached to the neighbouring Ben Youssef mosque, the medersa was a founded under one of Morocco's most illustrious rulers, the "Black Sultan" Abou

▼ FONDOUK, RUE AMESFAH

Fondouks

One of the most characteristic types of building in the Medina is the **fondouk** or caravanserai. Originally, *fondouks* were inns used by visiting merchants for storage and lodging when they were in Marrakesh to trade in its souks. All the *fondouks* have a courtyard in the middle surrounded by what were originally stables, while the upper level contains rooms which would have accommodated the merchants.

Today the *fondouks* are in varying states of repair; some have become private residences, others commercial premises. The doors to the courtyards are usually left open, and no one seems to mind if you wander in to have a look. Some *fondouks* date back to Saadian times (1520–1669), and boast fine woodcarving or stuccowork. There's a row of interesting fondouks on the south side of Rue Bab Debbagh, behind the Ben Youssef Medersa, and a whole series along Rue Amesfah, north of the Ben Youssef Mosque, as well as one directly opposite the Chrob ou Chouf fountain.

el Hassan (ruled 1331–49) of the Merenid dynasty. In the 1560s it was almost completely rebuilt under their successors the Saadians, whose intricate, Andalusian-influenced art dominates it. No surface is left undecorated, and the overall quality of its craftsmanship, whether in carved wood, stucco or *zellij*, is startling.

Inside the medersa, you reach the main court by means of a long outer corridor and a small entry vestibule. To the side of this are stairs to student cells, arranged round smaller internal courtyards on the upper floors. The central courtyard, its carved **cedar lintels** weathered almost flat on the most exposed side, is unusually large. Along two sides run wide, sturdy, columned arcades, and above them are some of the windows of the dormitory quarters. In the **prayer hall**, at the far end of the main court, the decoration is at its best preserved and most elaborate. Notable here, as in the courtyard's cedar carving, is a predominance of pine cone and palm motifs, especially around the *mihrab* (the horseshoe-arched niche indicating the direction of prayer), where their

clear protrusion from the rest of the frieze is a rarity in Moroccan stuccowork. The inscriptions are quotations from the Koran, the most common being its opening invocation: "In the name of God, the Compassionate, the Merciful".

Almost opposite the entrance to the Ben Youssef Medersa is the **Dar Bellarj**, a house built in the 1930s on the site of a *fondouk*. Now a cultural centre, with a small exhibition on irrigation, it's of no special interest, but charges passing tourists for entry as if it were.

Zaouia of Sidi Abdel Aziz el Harrar

Rue Mouassine. Sidi Abdel Aziz el Harrar (d.1508) was an Islamic scholar who – unusually among Marrakesh's Seven Saints (see box, p.78) – was actually born in Marrakesh, though he made his name in Fes. Among the Seven Saints' shrines, his *zaouia* is one of the smallest, but like the others it has a distinctive red and yellow pattern around the top, just below the roof, indicating that it would have been part of the pilgrimage circuit established here in the seventeenth century.

The Seven Saints of Marrakesh

Some two hundred holy men and women, known as **marabouts**, are buried in Marrakesh. Although the idea is considered slightly dubious in orthodox Islam, it's widely believed that praying to God at the tomb of a marabout attracts a special *beraka* (blessing). A marabout's tomb may thus become the centrepiece of a mosque called a **zaouia**, often the focus for a brotherhood of the marabout's followers, who usually belong to the mystic branch of Islam known as **Sufism**.

Marrakesh's seven most prominent marabouts, usually referred to in English as the "Seven Saints" of the city, have little in common aside from being buried here. One of them, Sidi Mohammed Ben Slimane, never even lived in Marrakesh – his body was brought here after his death. The most prominent, Sidi Bel Abbes, has become pretty much the city's patron saint.

Dar el Glaoui

Rue Dar el Bacha. Mon–Fri 9am–2pm. 10dh. Also called Dar el Bacha, this was the palace of **T'hami el Glaoui**, the despotic tribal leader – loved and feted by Europeans, feared and hated by Marrakshis – who ruled Marrakesh on behalf of the

▼ DAR EL GLAOUI

French during the colonial period. His extravagances were as legendary as his cruelty. When he died in 1956, a mob ransacked the palace, and the building is nowadays used by the Ministry of Culture. There isn't much to see today, though the caretaker may allow you in to admire the stucco-work of the two main courtyards.

Bab Doukkala Mosque

Rue Bab Doukkala. Serving the lively Bab Doukkala quarter, this *pisé* mosque with its elegant brick minaret was constructed in 1557–8 on the orders of Lalla Messaouda, mother of the Ahmed el Mansour, the most illustrious sultan of the Saadian dynasty. It is said that she originally intended to have it built in a different quarter, but the residents of this one managed to divert the builders and their materials to this site instead. On the main street in front of the mosque is the impressive three-bayed **Sidi el Hassan fountain**, now converted into a small art gallery.

Chrob ou Chouf Fountain

Rue Assouel, a little way north of Place de la Kissaria. This small sixteenth-century recessed fountain (its name means "drink and admire") is mainly notable for its carved cedar lintel, incorporating calligraphy and stalactite-like projections. Back in the days before people had running water at home, paying to put up a fountain was a pious act of charity, sanctioned by the Koran. Religious institutions and wealthy philanthropists had them installed to provide not only drinking water, but also a place to wash – most notably to perform the ritual ablutions demanded by the Koran before prayer, which is why so many of the surviving fountains are attached to mosques.

▲ RUE BAB DOUKKALA

Zaouia of Sidi Ben Salah

Place Ben Salah. This fourteenth-century holy man's tomb is one of the few important buildings in the Medina to have been put up under the Merenid dynasty, who had moved the Moroccan capital from Marrakesh to its rival city of Fes. The most prominent feature is the handsome **minaret**, covered with brilliant green tiles in a *darj w ktarf* pattern (see p.79). The square in front of the *zaouia* is usually pretty lively with fruit and vegetable sellers and other traders, and gives a flavour of Medina life without much influence from tourism.

The tanneries

Along and off Rue Bab Debbagh. Head east along Rue Bab Debbagh and you'll notice a rather unpleasant whiff in the air as you near Bab Debbagh, belying the proximity of the tanneries. One easy tannery to find is on the north side of the

street about 200m before Bab Debbagh, opposite the blue-tiled stand-up fountain, with another one about 200m further west.

The tanneries were sited at the edge of the city not only because of the smell, but also for access to water: a stream, the Oued Issil, runs just outside the walls. If you want to take a closer look at the **tanning process**, come in the morning, when the co-operatives are at work. The smell comes largely from the first stage, where the hides are soaked in a vat of pigeon droppings. The natural dyes traditionally used to colour the leather have largely been replaced by chemicals, many of them carcinogenic – a fact to remember when you see people standing waist-deep in them.

Bab Debbagh

Among the more interesting of Marrakesh's city gates, Bab Debbagh is supposedly

Almoravid in design, though over the years it must have been almost totally rebuilt. Passing through the gate, you become aware of its very real defensive purpose: three internal **chicanes** are placed in such a manner as to force anyone attempting to storm it to make several turns. Just before the gate, several shops on the left give good **views** over the tanneries from their roofs. Shopkeepers may invite you up, but agree the price first or you'll be mercilessly overcharged. Bus #5 outside the gate runs to and from the Koutoubia.

Bab el Khemis

This beautiful gate, originally Almoravid though rebuilt under the Almohads, is surrounded by concentric rings of decoration and topped with Christmas-tree-like castellations. Its name, meaning "Thursday Gate", is a reference to the market held outside, 300m to the north, past a marabout's tomb and a former cemetery, now landscaped as a little park. Thursday is when the main market is held (in the morning), but there are stalls out most days. It's mainly a local produce market, though the odd handicraft item does occasionally surface. Bus #5 connects Bab el Khemis with the Koutoubia.

Zaouia of Sidi Bel Abbes

Rue Bab Taghzout. The most important of Marrakesh's seven saints, **Sidi Bel Abbes** (b.1130) was a prolific performer of miracles, particularly famed for giving sight to the blind. The huge mosque that now houses his tomb, with a green-tiled roof and surrounding outbuildings,

▲ ZAOUIA OF SIDI BEN SLIMANE

dates largely from an early eighteenth-century reconstruction. It lies just north of **Bab Taghzout**, which is itself noteworthy in that it's not set within the city wall – in the eighteenth century, Sultan Mohammed Abdallah extended the Medina north to include the Sidi Bel Abbes quarter. As with all *zaouias*, non-Muslims are not allowed to enter the complex, but may take a look at it in from the outside. The foundation which runs the *zaouia* also owns much of the surrounding quarter and is engaged in charitable work, distributing food each evening to the blind.

Zaouia of Sidi Mohammed Ben Slimane

Rue Sidi Ben Slimane. The tomb of the fourteenth-century marabout **Sidi Mohammed Ben Slimane el Jazouli**, another of Marrakesh's seven saints, lies just southwest of Bab Tagzhout. His *zaouia* is not as impressive as that of Sidi Bel Abbes, though it has some interesting stucco-decorated doorways around it, most notably the one in the southeast corner.

Shops

Abdellatif Bellawi

56 & 103 Kissariat Lossta, between Souk el Kebir and Souk Attarine. Daily 9am–6pm (Fri till 5pm) Beads and bangles, yes, but we're talking class here: the beads are traditional Berber necklaces from the Atlas and the Sahara, and the bangles (mostly from the same regions) are chunky solid silver. There are more frivolous items too, like the cowrie-encrusted Gnaoua caps hanging up outside the door, plus rings and earrings, and woollen Berber belts.

Ait Aissa Mustapha

34 Souk Smata (Souk des Babouches). Daily 9am–6pm. There are any number of shops here selling traditional Moroccan slippers – worn with the back pushed down – but while neighbouring emporiums specialize in new-fangled designs, Mustapha sticks mainly to the classic yellow leather slipper, though with some tasteful variations – a pleasantly subdued grey for example – and some less tasteful ones, including a truly horrible snakeskin version. Prices start at around 200dh.

Artisanat Marocain

16–18 Souk Brâadia. Daily 10am–6pm The thuya (also spelt *thuja*) tree, which grows across the south of Morocco, is much prized: not only the wood but also the rootstock is hand-carved into beautiful sculptures, boxes and furniture, all sold here. Among the more popular items are chess and backgammon boards (inlaid with the yellow wood of citrus trees, and the same dyed black), solitaire sets and wooden jewel boxes. There are also some very elegant CD racks, and some great – in quality and scale – tables and chests. The boxes, incidentally, smell as good as they look – open one up and have a sniff.

Bazar du Sud

14 & 117 Souk des Tapis. Daily 8.30am–6.30pm. Carpets, carpets and carpets from all over the south of Morocco. Most are claimed to be old (if you prefer them spanking new, pop next

▼ CARPENTER AT WORK

door to Bazar Jouti at nos.16 & 119), and most are coloured with wonderful natural dyes such as saffron (yellow), cochineal (red) and indigo (blue). A large carpet could cost 2000dh, but you might be able to find a small rug for around 500dh.

El Meskini

152 Rahba Kedima, on the south side of the square. Daily 7am–10pm. Among the assorted apothecary shops on the south and west side of the Rahba Kedima, this one stands out for two reasons: firstly, it doesn't sell dubious animal products, and secondly, it's run by the genial Jamal, who'll patiently explain the wondrous properties of all the herbs, spices and scents he sells, whether you're after saffron (he sells two grades) or frankincense (ditto), herbs medicinal or culinary, *chebba* (alum), traditionally rubbed on cuts (especially shaving nicks), or poppy-petal rouge in an earthenware bowl.

Ensemble Artisanal

Av Mohammed V, midway between the Koutoubia and Bab Nkob ☎ 044 44 35 03. Mon–Sat 9am–1pm & 2.30–7pm, Sun 9am–1pm. This government-run complex of small arts and crafts shops holds a reasonable range of goods, notably leather, textiles and carpets. Shopping here is hassle-free, and the prices, which are more or less fixed, are a good gauge of the going rate if you intend to bargain elsewhere. At the back are a dozen or so workshops where you can watch young people learning a range of crafts including carpet-weaving.

Hasdi Hadj Abdelkarim

63 Souk Nejjarine, part of Souk el Kebir. Daily 9am–8.30pm. It's just a hole in the wall, but stop for a peek at Hadj Abdelkarim's small range of wooden spoons, hand-made in all sizes, and really quite charming in

▼ LINTEL OF THE MOUASSINE FOUNTAIN

their own small way. There are ladles for the eating of *harira*, spoons that you could stir your tea with, and non-spoon items too: old-fashioned washboards and even pairs of wooden scissors (for cutting fresh pasta, in case you wondered).

Hicham el Horre

12 Kissariat el Ahbasse, off Rue Souk Smarine. Daily 9am–9pm. The traditional ladies' (and some gents') clothing sold here is great for lounging about in at home. The finely tailored selection includes *jellabas* (with sleeves and a hood), kaftans (with sleeves but no hood), and *gandoras* (with neither sleeves nor hood), and there are also some nice embroidered tops to check out.

Kulchi

1 Rue des Ksour ☏ 062 64 97 83. Daily 9am–1.30pm & 4–7pm. Moroccan clothes for Western women is what this rather chic little boutique sells. The range isn't huge, but there are slinky kaftans, T-shirts with Moroccan-inspired designs, and diaphanous housecoats that you'll just love.

La Brocante

16 Souk Souaffine, off Souk el Kebir. Daily 9am–1pm & 4–7pm. A little shop with all sorts of antique curiosities: toys, watches, medals, enamelled metal signs, and what would be just bric-a-brac, but for the fact that it's clearly been chosen with a tasteful eye.

La Croix d'Agadez

Kissariat Mouassine, signposted off Rue Mouassine, just north of Rue des Ksour. Daily 8am–8pm. A shop full of all things Touareg. The shop's name refers to the Cross of Agadez, which has diamond-shaped arms and is named after the desert port in Niger. The cross symbolizes the south to the nomads of the Sahara: each tribe has its own variant of the cross as an emblem, and indeed much of the silver jewellery sold here is in the form of crosses. There's all sorts of other Saharan bric-a-brac too, from fossils and stone arrowheads through to whacking great amber beads.

Moulay el Arbi el Adlani

69 Souk el Kchachbia, west of the Almoravid Koubba. Daily 9.30am–7pm. The speciality here is mirrors, framed with mosaics of coloured glass. Costing 50dh and up, they're a little kitsch, to be sure, but sweetly so. The same shop has a small selection of *sebsis* (wooden pipes with a tiny bowl, used for smoking marijuana; they start at 15dh) and lanterns.

Patisserie Belkhabir and Patisserie Duniya

Souk Smarine Side by side, these shops specialize in traditional Moroccan sweetmeats, stuffed with nuts and drenched in syrup, and particularly popular during the holy month of Ramadan, when of course they are eaten by night. A half-kilo box of assorted sticky delights will set you back around 50dh.

Scarf shop

44 Kissariat Lossta. Daily 9am–6pm. Up Souk el Kebir (on the corner of the third alley on the left if you're heading north from the fork with Souk Attarine) is this little shop selling scarfs of cotton or silk – white and frilly, tie-dyed or plain. "This shop doesn't have a name," they insisted, but look for the scarfs and you'll see it soon enough (though the next shop along and the one opposite both sell scarfs too). Prices start at 10dh.

Restaurants

Dar Marjana

15 Derb Sidi Ali Tair, off Rue Bab Doukkala ☎044 38 51 10. Daily except Tues from 8pm. Advance booking only. Housed in an early nineteenth-century palace, said by some to be the most beautiful in the Medina. Look for the sign above the entrance to a passageway diagonally across the street from the corner of the Dar el Glaoui; take the passage and look for the green door facing you before a right turn. Among the tasty dishes they serve, two classics stand out: pastilla, a poultry (traditionally pigeon) pie spiced with cinnamon, originating from Fes in northern Morocco, and couscous *aux sept legumes*. The set menu costs 605dh.

▼ ENTERTAINMENT AT DAR MARJANA

Le Pavillon

47 Derb Zaouia ☎044 38 70 40. Daily except Tues from 8pm. Best approached from Rue Bab Doukkala, round the back of the Bab Doukkala mosque – look for the sign over the first archway on the right, head down the passage and it's the last door on the right. The restaurant is in a beautifully restored middle-class residence, with a tree-shaded patio and Berber wall hangings. Among the specialities of the French chef are lobster ravioli and a Grand Marnier soufflé. At around 300–400dh à la carte, it's more than worth the price.

Restaurant Yacout

79 Sidi Ahmed Soussi ☎044 38 29 00 or 29. Tues–Sun from 8pm. In a gorgeous old palace, the *Yacout* opened as a restaurant in 1987 with columns and fireplaces in super-smooth orange- and blue-striped *tadelakt* plaster, courtesy of American interior designer and Marrakesh resident Bill Willis. The owner, Mohammad Zkhiri, is also Marrakesh's British consul. The easiest way to get there is by *petit taxi* – the driver will usually walk you to the door. After a drink on the roof terrace, you move down into one of the intimate salons surrounding the courtyard for a selection of salads, followed by a tajine, then lamb couscous and (if you have room) dessert. The classic Moroccan tajine of chicken with preserved lemon and olive is a favourite here, but the fish tajine is also rated very highly. The cuisine has in the past received Michelin plaudits, though standards are beginning to slip as the tour groups move in. Booking ahead is advised. Count on 700dh per person.

Bars

Al'anbar

47 Rue Jebel Lakhdar. Daily 8pm–3am.
Drinking in this cavernous rich
people's hangout is an expensive
business, though pretty much
any kind of liquor you want is
available. The bar area is a huge
balcony overlooking the dining
area, as a theatre's upper circle
might overlook the stalls. It's
best to turn up late in the
evening when the place is
packed out and the dining area
becomes a dance floor.

The Ville Nouvelle

The downtown area of the Ville Nouvelle is **Guéliz**, whose main thoroughfare, **Avenue Mohammed V**, runs all the way down to the Koutoubia. It's in Guéliz that you'll find the the more upmarket stores and most of Marrakesh's nightlife. South of Guéliz, the **Hivernage** district was built as a garden suburb; it's where most of the city's newer tourist hotels are located. Though the Ville Nouvelle is hardly chock-a-block with attractions, it does have one must-see: the **Majorelle Garden**, east of Guéliz and just northwest of the Medina. West of Hivernage, the **Menara gardens** are less compelling, but they host an evening spectacle that you might enjoy.

▼ MAJORELLE GARDEN

Majorelle Garden (Jardin Bou Saf)

Off Av Yacoub el Mansour. Daily: April–Sept 8am–noon & 1–7pm; Sept–Nov 8am–noon & 1–5.30pm; Dec–Mar 8am–noon & 1–5pm. 15dh; no dogs or unaccompanied children allowed. The Majorelle Garden is a meticulously planned twelve-acre botanical garden, created in the 1920s and 1930s by French painter **Jacques Majorelle** (1886–1962), and now owned by fashion designer **Yves Saint Laurent**. The amazing feeling of tranquillity here is enhanced by verdant groves of bamboo, dwarf palm and agave, the cactus garden and the various lily-covered pools. The pavilion is painted in a striking cobalt blue – the colour of French workmen's overalls, so Majorelle claimed, though it seems to

RESTAURANTS, CAFÉS, BARS & CLUBS

Al Fassia	18	La Trattoria	15
Boule de Neige	1	Le Cantanzaro	11
Café des Negotiants	5	Marrakech Bodega	8
Café Le Siraoua	6	Mustan Club	2
Café Snack Le Sindibad	12	Paradise Disco	24
Café-Bar de l'Escale	14	Puerto Banus	21
Chesterfield Pub	10	Red House	23
Chez Jack'Line	4	Restaurant Le Jardin	19
Diamant Noir	20	Rotisserie de la Paix	16
Hotel Agdal	9	Samovar	3
Hotel Farouk	17	Solaris	13
La Taverne	7	VIP Club	22

▲ RELAXING AT BAB JEDID OLIVE GROVE

have improved in the Moroccan light.

In Majorelle's former studio, a **Museum of Islamic Arts** (15dh) exhibits Saint Laurent's fine personal collection of North African carpets, pottery, furniture and doors, and has one room devoted to Majorelle's engravings and paintings.

Menara gardens

Avenue de la Menara. Daily 8am–6pm. Free. A popular picnic spot for Marrakshi families, the Menara gardens couldn't be simpler to find: just follow the road from Bab Jedid, the gateway by the *Hotel La Mamounia*. Like the Agdal gardens (see p.67), the Menara was restored and its pavilions rebuilt in the mid-nineteenth century, though unlike the Agdal it is more olive grove than orchard. (If you want to get the feel of a true olive plantation, go to the nearby **Bab Jedid olive grove**, which makes a worthwhile stop on your way to or from the Menara.) The **pavilion** (*minzah*; 10dh admission) beside the Menara's central basin is said to have replaced an original Saadian structure.

Four days a week (except between early Jan and early Feb), the pool becomes the scene for a **Marvels and Reflections** show (Wed–Sat 9.45pm; 250dh or 400dh), featuring fireworks, dancers and acrobats. The ticket office (daily 9am–8pm) is at the park entrance; for further information, call ☏044 43 95 80 or check the show's website at ⓦwww.heritagevision.com.

Avenue Mohammed V

Named after the king who presided over Morocco's independence, Avenue Mohammed V is Marrakesh's main artery. It's on and around this boulevard that you'll find the city's main concentration of upmarket shops, restaurants and smart pavement cafés, and its junctions form the Ville Nouvelle's main centres of activity: **Place de la Liberté**, with its modern fountain; **Place 16 Novembre**, by the main post office; and **Place Abdelmoumen Ben Ali**, epicentre of Marrakesh's modern shopping zone and flanked by cafés. Looking back along Avenue Mohammed V from Guéliz to the Medina, on a clear day at least, you should see the Koutoubia rising in the distance.

The Théâtre Royal

40 Av de la France ☎044 43 15 16. At the time of writing, the new royal theatre and opera house had yet to be inaugurated, though with its Classical portico and dome, designed by Morocco's leading architect, **Charles Boccara**, it's already the most impressive piece of architecture in the Ville Nouvelle. When it does open its doors, it will serve as an exhibition hall as well as a performing arts centre.

Shops, markets and galleries

Amazonite

94 Bd El Mansour Eddahbi, Guéliz ☎044 44 99 26. Mon–Sat 9am–1pm & 3.30–7.30pm. The Marrakesh branch of a Casablanca store long known for its fine stock of *objets d'art*, Amazonite is the product of the owner's passion for rare and beautiful things. Most of the pieces are antique, with a hefty proportion comprised of jewellery; if asked, staff explain each item with charm and grace.

Jeff de Bruges

17 Rue de la Liberté, Guéliz ☎044 43 02 49. Mon–Sat 9am–1pm & 3–7.30pm. This Belgian firm sells fine chocolate flown in all the way from Bruges – not authentically Moroccan, but very nice indeed. One hundred grams of assorted lusciousness will set you back 44dh.

La Gallerie Bleu

119 Av Mohammed V, Guéliz ☎044 42 00 80. Tues–Sun 10am–1pm & 4–8pm. The most chic of Marrakesh's art galleries, specializing in modern paintings from Morocco and abroad. The selection of works, mostly very abstract, is small but well laid out.

PLACES The Ville Nouvelle

▼ THE NEW THÉÂTRE ROYAL

▲ PLACE 16 NOVEMBRE

Librairie Chatr

19 Av Mohammed V, Guéliz ☎044 44 79 97. Mon–Sat 8am–1pm & 3–8pm. This bookshop and stationer's sells mainly French titles, most notably books on trekking, skiing and rock carvings in the High Atlas, which are right at the back under "Tourisme". There's also a shelf of English-language material, mostly classics, at the back on the right.

Librairie d'Art ACR

Résidence Taïb, 55 Bd Mohammed Zerktouni, Guéliz ☎044 44 67 92. Mon–Sat 9am–12.30pm & 3–7pm. This bookshop stocks the beautiful ACR range of French art and coffee-table books, including several on Marrakesh and Moroccan interior design, as well as on subjects such as architecture, textiles and jewellery.

L'Orientaliste

11 & 15 Rue de la Liberté, Guéliz ☎044 43 40 74. Mon–Sat 9am–12.30pm & 3–7.30pm. Specializing in rather chic North African-style home furnishings, L'Orientaliste also does a fine line in limited Moroccan pop-art screen-prints by local artist Hassan Hajjaj. At no. 15 it's mainly furniture that's

stocked, while at no. 11 they concentrate on smaller items, including glassware and perfume.

Lun'art Gallery

24 Rue Moulay Ali, Guéliz ☎044 44 72 66. Daily 9am–12.30pm & 4–8pm. Despite its name, this is really an interior design shop, with a selection of furniture and accessories for the home. Nonetheless, it's the paintings that most inspire, modern, lively and full of strong Moroccan characters.

Municipal market

Av Mohammed V. Daily 8am–1.15pm & 4–7.30pm. A far cry from the markets in the Medina, and much more like those of Continental Europe, this is where well-heeled Marrakshis come for fresh fish and meat, fruit and veg. There's a whole section devoted to cut flowers, plus an assortment of souvenir stalls selling pottery, fossils and tourist tat, not to mention a delicatessen and two butchers specializing in horsemeat.

Place Vendôme

141 Av Mohammed V, Guéliz ☎044 43 52 63. Mon–Sat 9am–12.30pm & 3–7.30pm. Morocco leather is of

course world famous, and you'll certainly find it here, along with some very sumptuous soft leather and suede, in the form of bags, belts, wallets and clothes. Purses start at 100dh, and there are some very stylish ladies' garments – jackets, coats and dresses – at around 3000dh.

Cafés

Boule de Neige

20 Rue de Yougoslavie, just off Place Abdelmoumen Ben Ali. Daily 5am–11pm. This lively patisserie serves Continental and American breakfasts and all-day snacks, as well as good ice cream and a range of coffees. It also serves toast with *amalou* – a tasty paste made of honey, almonds and the exquisite, nutty oil of the argan tree, found only in the south of Morocco. In the evenings, there's live Moroccan pop music, too.

Café des Negotiants

Place Abdelmoumen Ben Ali. Daily 6am–midnight. Slap bang on the busiest corner in Guéliz, this grand café is the place to sit out on the pavement and really feel that you're in the heart of modern Marrakesh. It's also an excellent venue in which to spend the morning over a coffee, with a choice of different croissants (plain, chocolate, almond), or even crepes and fruit juice, to accompany your fix of caffeine.

Café Le Siraoua

20 Bd Mohammed Zerktouni, next to the Colisée cinema. Daily 4am–11.30pm. Near the CTM bus depot, this café is a favourite spot for breakfast, serving croissants, orange juice and coffee. There's a choice of seats: out on the pavement, or in a busy area with a TV, or in a larger, quieter dining area, decorated with orientalist prints.

Café Snack Le Sindibad

Résidence Elite, Av Mohammed V. Daily 24hr. Serves inexpensive food – salad and tajine with dessert will set you back around 50dh. Rather seedy, it's mostly of interest for being open when everything else is shut.

▾ CAFÉ SNACK LE SINDIBAD

Solaris

170 Av Mohammed V. Daily 7am–11pm. This bright establishment under a neon sign looks just a tad more modern and sophisticated than your average Marrakesh coffee house, with tiled floors and mirror panels behind the bar. The basketwork chairs and tables are just right to relax at with your coffee and croissant while you watch the comings and goings along the boulevard.

Restaurants

Al Fassia

232 Av Mohammed V ☎044 43 40 60. Daily noon–2.30pm & 7–11pm. Truly Moroccan – both in decor and cuisine – and specializing in dishes from the country's culinary capital of Fes, starting with that great classic, pastilla, followed with a choice of six

▾ULYSSES, CHEZ JACK'LINE

different lamb tajines. There's a lunchtime set menu for around 150dh, but dinner will cost twice that. The ambience and service are superb.

Chez Jack'Line

63 Av Mohammed V, near Place Abdelmoumen Ben Ali ☎044 44 75 47. Daily noon–2.30pm & 7–11pm. French, Italian and Moroccan dishes are all served here under the skilful direction of the indefatigable Jack'Line Pinguet and the beady eye (upstairs) of Ulysses, her parrot. You can eat splendidly for 150dh à la carte – top choices are the steaks and pasta dishes, including superb cannelloni – or go for the good-value 80dh set menu based on couscous or tajine.

Hotel Farouk

66 Av Hassan II ☎044 43 19 89. Daily 5am–10pm. From noon the hotel restaurant offers an excellent-value 50dh set menu with soup, salad, couscous, tajine or brochettes, followed by fruit, ice cream or home-made yoghurt. Alternatively, tuck in to one of their excellent wood-oven pizzas.

La Taverne

22 Bd Mohammed Zerktouni ☎044 44 61 26. Daily 12.30–3pm & 7–10.30pm. As well as a drinking tavern, this is also a pretty decent restaurant – in fact, it claims to be the oldest in town – where you can dine on French and Moroccan fare indoors or in a lovely tree-shaded garden. The 90dh four-course set menu is very good value indeed.

La Trattoria

179 Rue Mohammed el Bekal ☎044 43 26 41, ⊛www.latrattoriamarrakesh .com. Mon–Sat 7–11.30pm. The best Italian food in town, with

impeccable but friendly service and utterly excellent cooking. The restaurant is located in a 1920s house decorated by the acclaimed American designer Bill Willis. As well as freshly made pasta, steaks and escalopes, there are specialities like *tagliata de boeuf* – made with beef, capers and herbs from the Atlas mountains – plus a wonderful tiramisú to squeeze in for afters.

Le Cantanzaro

50 Rue Tarik Ibn Ziad ☎044 43 37 31. Mon–Sat noon–2.30pm & 7.30–11.30pm. Behind the municipal market, near the *Hôtel Toulousain*, this is one of the city's most popular Italian restaurants, crowded at lunchtime with Marrakshis, expats and tourists. Specialities include *saltimbocca alla romana* and rabbit in mustard sauce, and there's *crème brûlée* to round off with. You're strongly advised to book or you could wait for a while for a table.

The Red House

Boulevard el Yarmouk, opposite the Medina wall, Hivernage ☎044 43 70 40 or 044 43 70 41, ☻www .theredhouse-marrakech.com. Daily noon–2.30pm & 7.30–10.30pm.

You'll need to reserve ahead to eat at this palatial riad (also known as *Dar el Ahmar*), beautifully decorated in stucco and *zellij*. There's a Moroccan set menu (450dh), featuring pigeon pastilla and lamb tajine with prunes and sesame, or you can dine à la carte on the likes of prawn and langouste ravioli or sashimi of trout and John Dory.

Restaurant Le Jardin

Rue Oum Rabia, on a side road off Av Mohammed V (look for the *Pizza Hut* on the opposite side of the avenue) ☎044 44 82 10. Mon–Sat 11.30am–2.30pm & 7–11.30pm. French and Italian cuisine in a jolly little place with modern decor, pink walls and little lamps on each table. The menu consists mainly of wood-oven pizzas, fresh pasta and classy meat dishes such as grills, entrecotes and *osso bucco*, for around 160dh per head, not including wine.

Restaurant Puerto Banus

Rue Ibn Hanbal, opposite the Police Headquarters and Royal Tennis Club ☎044 44 65 34. Daily noon–3pm & 7.30pm–midnight. A Spanish fish restaurant – though French-managed – with specialities such as gazpacho and paella, and

▼ AVENUE MOHAMMED V

▲ PETITS TAXIS

oysters introduced from Japan to Oualidia on the Moroccan coast. There's also a good selection of French and Moroccan dishes, including seafood pastilla. Count on 200dh per head without wine.

Rotisserie de la Paix

68 Rue Yougoslavie, alongside the former cinema Lux-Palace ☎ 044 43 31 18, ✆ www.restaurant-diaffa.ma. Daily noon–3pm & 7–11pm. An open-air grill, established in 1949, specializing in mixed grills barbecued over wood, usually with a fish option for non-meat-eaters, all served either in a salon with a roaring fire in winter, or in the shaded garden in summer. Fish couscous is served on Fridays.

Bars

Café-Bar de l'Escale

Rue Mauritanie, just off Av Mohammed V. Daily 11am–10.30pm. An old-school all-male Moroccan drinking den which has been going since 1947. It's known for good bar snacks, such as fried fish or merguez sausages – you could even come here for lunch or dinner (there's a dining area at the back). Not recommended for unaccompanied women.

Chesterfield Pub

Gallerie Merchande, 119 Av Mohammed V. Daily 10am–midnight. Next to the *Nassim Hotel*, this supposedly English pub – it's nothing of the sort – is one of Marrakesh's more sophisticated watering holes, with a cosy if rather smoky bar area, all soft seats and muted lighting. There's also a more relaxed, open-air poolside terrace to lounge about on with your draught beer or cocktail of a summer evening.

Hotel Agdal

1 Bd Mohammed Zerktouni. Daily 5.30pm–12.30am. The bar here is pretty cosy as Moroccan drinking holes go, and one where women should feel reasonably comfortable despite the presence of a few prostitutes.

You can sit at the bar or more discreetly at one of the tables.

Marrakech Bodega

23 Rue de la Liberté; daily 6pm–1am. A welcome addition to Marrakesh's drinking scene, a fun, *rancho*-style bar with red wooden beams, Latin music, tapas and draught San Miguel on tap. Members of both sexes can enjoy themselves here without the boorish drunkenness of your average Moroccan bar.

Samovar

145 Rue Mohammed el Bekal, Guéliz, next to the *Hôtel Oudaya*. Daily 10am–11pm. An old-school, low-life drinking den, a male hangout with bar girls in attendance. The customers get more and more out of it as the evening progresses – if you want to see the underbelly of Morocco's drinking culture, this is where to come. Definitely not recommended for women visitors, however.

Nightclubs

Diamant Noir

Rue Oum er Bia, behind *Hôtel Marrakesh*, Guéliz. Daily 11pm–3am. Look for the signpost on Av Mohammed V to find this lively dance club where Western pop and disco alternate with Algerian and Moroccan *raï* music – it's the latter that really fills the dance floor. There are two bars, quite a sophisticated range of drinks (the 100dh entry ticket includes one), and a mainly young crowd, a mixture of couples, singles and a gay contingent.

Mustan Club

68 Bd Zerktouni, Guéliz. Daily 11pm–3am. Don't be put off by the rather scraggy flashing neon light over the entrance – this may not be the poshest joint in town (in fact it's a bit of a dive), but it's got to be the most good-natured and the least pretentious. Drunken bonhomie reigns as a mixed crowd of all ages do their thing to the sound of a four-piece Arabic folk band with female vocalist, interspersed with disco, pop and even hip-hop records. No one stands on ceremony and a good time is generally had by all. The 50dh entry ticket includes your first drink.

Paradise Disco

Hotel Kempinski, Bd El Mansour Eddahbi, Hivernage. Daily midnight–4am. A smart and trendy club – also called *Club Calypso* – that tries to be reasonably exclusive. The clientele is mainly well-heeled young Moroccans (plus tourists staying at the attached five-star hotel), the music Euro-disco with a few local sounds thrown in. The seating area is big, the dance floor surprisingly small.

VIP Club

Place de la Liberté, Guéliz. Daily midnight–4am. Purple and turquoise neon lights lead you down the gullet-like entrance to this two-level club where an Arabic folk band plays while bright young things, a sprinkling of tourists and some rather persistent prostitutes waggle their booties to a mix of Western sounds on the main dance floor – not what you expected Marrakesh to be like at all.

Around the city

The countryside around Marrakesh is some of the most beautiful in Morocco. The High Atlas mountains that make such a spectacular backdrop to the city are even more impressive when you're actually among them. For a spot of hiking, or even skiing, they're easy enough to reach in an hour or two by grand taxi (see p.119) from the gare routière de Bab er Robb, 2km southwest of the Jemaa el Fna. Otherwise, you can get a peaceful respite from the full-on activity of Marrakesh's streets by heading to the palmery, or oasis, just outside the city.

The palmery

Northeast of Marrakesh between the Route de Fès (N8) and the Route de Casablanca (N9). Marrakesh's **palmery** is dotted with the villas of prosperous Marrakshis, and also boasts a golf course and a couple of luxury hotels. The clumps of date palms look rather windswept, but the palmery does have a certain tranquility, and it's several degrees cooler than the Medina, which makes it a particular attraction in summer.

The most popular route through the oasis is the **Circuit de la Palmeraie**, which meanders through the trees and villas from the Route de Fès to the Route de Casablanca. The classic way to see it is by *calèche* (see p.120), but you could get there by ordinary public transport, taking bus #17 or #26 to the Route de Fès turn-off, and bus #1 back from the Route de Casablanca (or vice versa).

▼ A CALÈCHE RIDE TO THE PALMERY

Trekking in the Atlas

You could spend many days trekking in the High Atlas mountains that begin just south of Marrakesh. There are trails to suit the casual hiker, and routes that can be covered in a day. The easiest walks take in pretty valleys spread with a patchwork of little fields dotted with walnut trees. With the right equipment, clothing and supplies, it's even possible to climb **Jebel Toubkal** (4167m), North Africa's highest peak, though this is not an ascent to be taken lightly.

The easiest base for Atlas treks and hikes is **IMLIL**, which costs 25dh per person to reach by *grand taxi*. Imlil has a few good places to stay – the basic *CAF Refuge* (dorm beds 52dh, less for Club Alpin Français or Hostelling International members), the decent *Hotel-Café Soleil* (☎044 48 56 22; double rooms from 100dh including breakfast), and the upmarket, British-run *Kasbah du Toubkal* (☎044 48 56 11, ☻www.kasbahdutoubkal .com; double rooms from €130dh including breakfast). Easy hikes from here include the mule trail to **Asni** (6hr), where there's transport back to Marrakesh. An alternative route is the short trek to **Tachdirt**

▲ ATLAS MOUNTAIN VILLAGE

(3–4hr), which has another *CAF Refuge*. From Tachdirt, it's a day's trek down to **Setti Fatma** in the beautiful **Ourika Valley**, where there's transport back to Marrakesh. Another option from Tachdirt is the superb day's walk to **Timichi**, where you can stay at a *gîte d'étape* – a private house where there are rooms for rent (expect to pay 30–50dh per person), then on the following day take a six-hour walk down to Setti Fatma, or across to Oukaïmeden (see p.98), or a seven- to nine-hour route down to Asni.

To hire a guide in Marrakesh (expect to pay 250dh per day),

Every year in mid-August, Setti Fatma holds a **moussem** dedicated to the local saint whom the village is named after. The saint's tomb stands by the river on the way to the waterfalls above the village. Although the *moussem* is religious in origin, it is just as much a fair and market, attracting Sufi mystics as well as performers like those of Marrakesh's Jemaa el Fna. All in all it's also an enjoyable family occasion, with adults and children from the village and the surrounding area taking part.

you could try the office of the Mountain Guides' Association (Association Nationale des Guides et Accompagnateurs en Montagne du Maroc – ANGAMM), just off Jemaa el Fna at Immeuble 12, Appt 6, Rue Bani Marine (Ⓣ044 42 75 80, Ⓔangamm45@hotmail.com). Among hotels, the *Hotel Ali* (see p.110) is one of the best places to get information and arrange guides.

Skiing in Oukaïmeden

Morocco may not strike you as a country to go skiing in, but the High Atlas village of **OUKAÏMEDEN** (referred to as "Ouka" for short), 74km from Marrakesh, has 20km of runs to suit skiers and snowboarders at all levels. One of the ski lifts here was at one time the highest in the world, reaching 3273m. It's now supplemented by four shorter lifts, and it is possible to reach even higher terrain using donkeys – an option you don't get at Aspen or St Moritz. There are nursery and intermediate runs on the lower slopes for the less advanced, and off-piste skiing and snowboarding are also available.

Snowfall and snow cover are variable, with **conditions** generally at their best in late January and early February. The slopes are sometimes icy early and wet by afternoon, and pistes are not tremendously well cared for (beware of hidden rocks), but not having to queue in the mornings lets you get in plenty of skiing.

In winter, *grands taxis* serve Oukaïmeden from Marrakesh (60dh). If you're heading up on a day-trip, you can arrange both legs of the journey at the outset for 85dh per person, there and back. As for chartering a taxi, expect to pay 500dh there and back. A snowplough keeps access roads open in the skiing season (December to April inclusive), after which the ski lifts close even if conditions are still good.

Ski passes cost just 50dh, and lessons are available from local instructors. You can rent **equipment** from shops near *Chez Juju* for around 150dh a day. There are several **hotels**, including the excellent *Chez Juju* on the main road in the centre of the village (Ⓣ044 45 90 05; 680dh for a double room with full board), and the four-star *Kenzi Louka* at the top of the village (Ⓣ044 31 90 80 or 86, Ⓦwww.kenzi-hotels.com; 1124dh half board).

▼ATLAS TREKKING

Essaouira

Around 170km west of Marrakesh, the seaside resort of Essaouira has had a special relationship with tourists since the 1960s, when its popularity as a hippy resort attracted the likes of Jimi Hendrix. Since then it has become a centre for artists and windsurfers, but despite increasing numbers of foreign visitors it remains one of the most laid-back, likeable towns in Morocco. Its whitewashed and blue-shuttered houses, enclosed by spectacular **battlements**, provide a colourful backdrop to a long, sandy beach.

The Medina

The fairy-tale **ramparts** around Essaouira's Medina may look medieval, but they actually date from the reign of eighteenth-century sultan Sidi Mohammed Ben Abdallah, who commissioned a French military architect named Theodore Cornut to build a new town on a site previously occupied by a series of forts. The result is a walled Medina with unique blend of Moroccan and French street layout, combining a crisscross of main streets with a labyrinth of alleyways between them.

At the heart of the Medina are the main **souks**, centred on two arcades either side of Rue Mohammed Zerktouni. On the northwest side is the **spice souk**, where culinary aromatics join incense, traditional cosmetics and even natural aphrodisiacs billed as "herbal Viagra". Across the way, the **jewellers' souk** sells not just gems but also all kinds of crafts. The decline in the jewellery trade was mainly due to the departure of the Jewish community, who once provided most of Essaouira's goldsmiths and silversmiths and made up

▼ TAKING SHADE, ESSAOUIRA

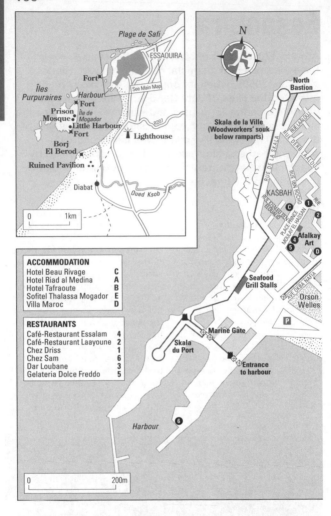

ACCOMMODATION

Hotel Beau Rivage	C
Hotel Riad al Medina	A
Hotel Tafraoute	B
Sofitel Thalassa Mogador	E
Villa Maroc	D

RESTAURANTS

Café-Restaurant Essalam	4
Café-Restaurant Laayoune	2
Chez Driss	1
Chez Sam	6
Dar Loubane	3
Gelateria Dolce Freddo	5

Getting to Essaouira

Reaching Essaouira from Marrakesh by public transport is a cinch, though the journey time means you'll probably want to stay overnight. The cheapest way is to get a **bus** (15 daily; 3hr 30min; around 50dh) from the *gare routière* (see p.125). You arrive at Essaouira's bus station, a ten-minute walk outside Essaouira's Bab Doukkala, or a short *petit taxi* ride from the Medina (5dh). A faster and more comfortable bus service is provided by **Supratours** (2 or 3 daily; 2hr 30min; 55dh), leaving from Marrakesh's train station and arriving at Bab Marrakesh in Essaouira. At the time of writing, departures from Marrakesh were at 11am and 7pm. It's usually no prob-

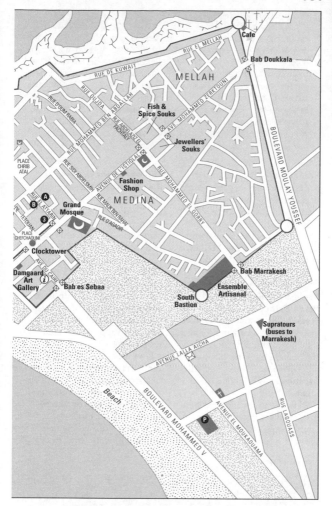

lem to get seats on Supratours services, though bear in mind that when they are busy (before and after Eid el Kebir, and during the Gnaoua Music Festival at the end of June for example), priority is given to train passengers requiring an onward connection. Finally, there are **grand taxis** to Essaouira (2hr 30min; 70dh) from the rank behind Marrakesh's *gare routière*; in Essaouira they might drop you in town itself, though they actually operate from a yard by the bus station.

Essaouira's **tourist office** is located on Avenue du Caire (Mon–Fri 9am–noon & 3–6.30pm, June to mid-Sept Mon–Sat 9am–1pm & 3–7pm; ☎044 78 35 32).

The Gnaoua Festival

Essaouira's main annual event is the Gnaoua and World Music Festival (@www.festival-gnaoua.co.ma), usually held on the last weekend in June. The festival focuses chiefly on the music of the **Gnaoua**, a Moroccan Sufi brotherhood with West African roots going back to the days of slavery. Stages are set up in the plaza between Place Prince Moulay el Hassan and the port, and outside Bab Marrakesh, and performers come from Tangier, Marrakesh and, of course, Essaouira, with special guests from Europe, the Caribbean and West Africa, in particular Senegal. During the festival, which attracts as many as 200,000 people, you can expect hotels and transport to be full, so book well ahead if possible.

around half of the town's population. They began to leave after the Arab–Israeli conflict made their position here difficult, and the northern quarter of the Medina where they mainly lived, the **Mellah**, is now the poorest and most run-down part of town.

The western part of the Medina, the **Kasbah**, centres on **Place Prince Moulay el Hassan**. This is the town's main square, where locals and tourists alike linger over a mint tea or a coffee and enjoy the lazy pace of life. The square to the south, the **Mechouar**, is bounded by an imposing wall topped by a clocktower and flanked by palm trees, in whose shade townspeople often take a breather from the heat of the day.

The Skala de la Ville

Rue de Skala. Daily sunrise–sunset. Free. The city's northern bastion, the **Skala de la Ville**, commands panoramic views across the Medina and out to sea. It was one of the main Essaouira locations used in Orson Welles's 1952 screen version of *Othello*. Along the top are a collection of European **cannons**, presented to Sidi Mohammed Ben Abdallah by ambitious nineteenth-century merchants.

Down below, built into the ramparts along the Rue de Skala, you can see some of the town's many **marquetry** and **woodcarving** workshops, where artisans produce amazingly painstaking and beautiful pieces from **thuya**

▼ BOATYARD, ESSAOUIRA

▲ THE SKALA DU PORT

wood. With total justice, they claim that their products are the best of their type in the country. Elsewhere, in town, Afalkay Art (see p.104) is a good place to get an idea of prices and the range of goods available.

The Skala du Port

Daily 8.30am–noon & 2.30–6pm. 10dh. The **Skala du Port**, the square sea bastion by the harbour, topped by lookout posts in each of its four corners, is worth popping into for the **views** from the ramparts. Looking east, you have a brilliant vista along the seaward side of the walled city, especially pretty towards sunset, when it's often bathed in a pinkish glow. To the south, the Skala overlooks the bustling **port area**, where local wooden fishing boats are built or repaired, and where the fishing fleet brings in the day's catch.

The beach

The main **beach**, to the south of town, extends for miles. On its early reaches, the main activity is **football** a game is virtually always in progress, and at weekends there's a full-scale local league.

The wind here can be a bit remorseless for sunbathing in spring and summer, but it's perfect for **windsurfing**, and Essaouira is Morocco's number one windsurfing resort. Equipment can be rented on the beach at Magic Fun Afrika (☎061 10 37 77, ✉magicfunafrika @hotmail.com), 500m south of the Medina, or a little further down the beach at Ocean Vagabond (☎061 34 71 02, ✉oceanvagabond@directwind .com), both closed from December to March. The water is cool enough to make a wetsuit essential year-round.

If you head further along the beach, past the football and the crowds, you'll pass the riverbed of the Oued Ksob (which can't be crossed at high tide) and come upon the ruins of an eighteenth-century circular fort, the **Borj el Berod**, which almost looks as though it is melting into the sand. Local legend has it that Jimi Hendrix played impromptu concerts here for fellow hippies, but the story that it inspired his "Castles Made of Sand" is definitely apocryphal, as the track was recorded long before he came to town.

▲ THE SKALA DU PORT

Shops and galleries

Afalkay Art

9 Place Prince Moulay el Hassan ☎044 47 60 89. Daily 9am–8pm. A vast emporium of thuya marquetry and woodcarving, with a massive selection of boxes, chess and backgammon sets, furniture, sculptures and carvings (some of which are from Senegal rather than local). This place also has marked, fixed prices, so it's a good place to see what's available and how much it's going to cost, even if you end up doing your shopping elsewhere.

Fashion Shop

24 Av Sidi Mohammed Ben Abdallah. Daily 10am–1pm & 3–7pm. Hippy-style clothing is one of Essaouira's best buys, and this little boutique does a good line in tunics and drawstring trousers, mostly white and cream-coloured, and beautifully cool in Morocco's sometimes relentless heat.

Galerie d'Art Frederic Damgaard

Av Oqba Ibn Nafia, Mechouar ☎044 78 44 46. Daily 10am–1pm & 3–7pm. Essaouira's artists have made a name for themselves in both Morocco and Europe, and those whose paintings and sculptures are exhibited here have developed their own highly distinctive styles, in some cases attracting an entourage of imitators. The gallery is run by a Danish furniture designer, whose own work uses traditional thuya techniques in an imaginative, modern context. Damgaard also has an *atelier* at 2 Rue El Hijalli, just off Place Chefchaouni, which is also worth a look around.

Cafés and ice-cream parlours

Chez Driss

10 Rue Hajjali, just off Place Prince Moulay el Hassan. Daily 9am–6pm. Well established as one of Essaouira's most popular meeting places, serving delicious fresh pastries and coffee in a quiet leafy courtyard. It's the ideal spot for a leisurely breakfast.

Gelateria Dolce Freddo

On the plaza between Place Prince Moulay el Hassan and the port. Daily until 9pm. Delicious Italian ice creams at just 5dh a scoop – the tiramisú flavour is to die for.

Restaurants

Café-Restaurant Essalam

Place Prince Moulay el Hassan. Daily noon–11pm. Though the choice is a little bit limited at this popular budget eating place, they do have the cheapest set menus in town (28–40dh), as well as tajines and Continental breakfasts (20dh).

Café-Restaurant Laayoune

4 Rue Hajjali ☏044 47 46 43. Daily noon–3pm & 7–11pm. Good for moderately priced tajines and other Moroccan staples in a relaxed setting with friendly service, though you may find the low tables and divan seating a bit awkward. You can eat à la carte (main dishes around 35dh) or choose from a range of tajine- and couscous-based set menus (45–72dh).

Chez Sam

In the fishing port ☏044 47 65 13. Daily noon–3pm & 7–11pm. An Essaouira institution – a wooden shack, built like a boat, set seductively right by the waterfront in the harbour. Service can be a bit hit-and-miss but the portions are generous, the fish is usually cooked pretty well, there's beer and wine, and you can watch the fishing boats through the portholes. The best fish is only available à la carte (main dishes around 80dh), but there's a good-value set menu for 85dh, or one with lobster for 200dh.

Dar Loubane

24 Rue du Rif, near Place Chefchaouni ☏044 47 62 96. Daily noon–3pm & 7–11pm. On the ground floor patio of an attractive eighteenth-century mansion, this upmarket restaurant serves up fine Moroccan and French cuisine (main dishes around 80dh) among an eccentric collection of interesting, sometimes rather kitsch odds and ends that decorate the walls and the courtyard. There's live Gnaoua music on Saturday evening, when it's advisable to make a booking.

Seafood grill stalls

Off Place Prince Moulay el Hassan, on the way to the port. Daily noon–10pm. An absolute must if you're staying in Essaouira is a meal at one of these makeshift grill stalls, with wooden tables and benches laid out overlooking the sea. Each displays a selection of freshly caught fish, prawns, squid, lobster and other seafood delights – all you need to do is check the price (haggling is *de rigueur*) and select the marine denizens of your choice, which are whisked off to the barbecue to reappear on your plate a few minutes later. Despite the initial hustle for custom, the atmosphere is relaxed and standards high. Expect to pay 30dh for a simple fish supper, 150dh for one featuring lobster or langouste.

▼SEAFOOD SPREAD AT GRILL STALL

Accommodation

Hotel Beau Rivage

4 Place Prince Moulay el Hassan ☎044 47 59 25. This former backpackers' hotel has been completely refurbished and has taken a step upmarket. It has an enviable position right on the main square – which also means that rooms at the front can be a bit noisy at times. There's a variety of charming en-suite rooms; doubles are 250dh without breakfast.

Hotel Riad al Medina

9 Rue Attarine ☎044 47 27 27, ☏044 47 52 27, ✇www.riadalmadina.com. A former palatial mansion built in 1871, this had fallen on hard times by the 1960s and become a budget hotel for hippies. Guests supposedly included Jimi Hendrix (in room 13 according to some stories, room 28 say others), as well as Frank Zappa, the Jefferson Airplane and Cat Stevens. Now refurbished, it has

▾ MARINE GATE

bags of character and helpful staff but it's still rather rustic in some respects (the plumbing can be temperamental for example). Double rooms start at 664dh excluding breakfast.

Hotel Tafraout

7 Rue de Marrakesh ☎044 47 62 76. A spotless little budget hotel with friendly staff and comfortable rooms, some en suite, though not all have outside windows. There's hot water in the evenings only, but right next door there are public hot showers for both sexes. Doubles start at 150dh without breakfast.

Sofitel Thalassa Mogador

Bd Mohammed V ☎044 47 90 00, ☏044 47 90 80, ✇www.sofitel.com. The most expensive hotel in Essaouira by a very long chalk, featuring a pool, two bars, two restaurants and a thalassotherapy centre (if a swim in the sea isn't sufficient). One is room adapted for wheelchair users. Double rooms are 2234dh, not including breakfast.

Villa Maroc

10 Rue Abdallah Ben Yassin, just inside the Medina wall near the clocktower ☎044 47 61 47, ☏044 47 58 06, ✇www.villa-maroc.com. An upmarket riad comprising two old houses converted into a score of rooms and suites. Established long before riads became trendy, it's decorated with the finest Moroccan materials and even has its own hammam. The *Villa* is accessible only on foot, though there are porters on hand to carry your luggage from the car park in Place Orson Welles. Most of the year you will need to book several months ahead to stay here. Double rooms 850dh including breakfast.

Accommodation

Accommodation

Accommodation

Marrakesh has a good selection of accommodation in all price ranges. The big new trend in town is the **riad** or *maison d'hôte* – there are now dozens of riads in Marrakesh, mostly in the **Medina**. Originally, a riad meant a house built around a patio garden (in fact, "riad" correctly refers to the garden rather than the house); *maison d'hôte* is, of course, "guest house" in French. In the local tourist industry, however, both terms are used, pretty much interchangeably, for a house done up to accommodate tourists.

Riads range from plain and simple lodgings in a Moroccan family home to restored old mansions with classic decor. Most common are Moroccan houses which have been done up by European owners to look like something from an interior-design magazine, with swimming pools in the patio and jacuzzis on the roof. At their best, riads allow you to stay in comfort in a Medina home, often with the family who live in it, which can be a good way to get a feel for Moroccan life. Most riads are expensive, however, compared

Seasons vary slightly from establishment to establishment, but in general, **high season** for Marrakesh accommodation means March–May plus September and October, as well as Christmas and New Year. The rates quoted here – which include **breakfast** unless otherwise stated – are for the **cheapest double room** in high season; the rest of the year, you can expect prices to be anything from ten to fifty percent cheaper. However, if you intend to visit over **Christmas/New Year** period, note that this represents an exceptional peak within high season, when rates at some hotels can be as much as fifty percent higher than in the rest of the high season.

with hotels, and a lot are seriously overpriced, so it pays to shop around and be choosy.

As for **hotels**, the modern three-, four- and five-star establishments are concentrated in **Guéliz** and **Hivernage**, the latter district home to the big international chains like *Sheraton* and *Meridien*. However, the very poshest establishments, such as the *La Mamounia* and the *Maison*

Riad-booking agencies

Marrakesh Medina 102 Rue Dar el Bacha, Northern Medina ☎044 44 24 48, ℱ044 39 10 71, ℻www.marrakech-medina.com. A firm that's actually in the business of doing up riads as well as renting them out, with a reasonable selection in all price ranges.

Marrakesh Riads Dar Cherifa, 8 Derb Charfa Lakbir, Northern Medina ☎044 42 64 63, ℱ044 42 65 11. A small agency with only half a dozen riads, but trying to keep it chic and authentic.

Riads au Maroc 1 Rue Mahjoub Rmiza, Guéliz ☎044 43 19 00, ℱ044 43 17 86, ℻www.riadomaroc.com. One of the first and biggest, riad agencies, with lots of choice in all price categories.

Arabe, offering palatial style along with the usual de luxe facilities (air conditioning, a swimming pool and gourmet dining), are back in the **Medina**. This is also where you'll find the most characterful mid-range hotels, usually in refurbished houses with en-suite rooms priced at 300–400dh. Mostly in the Medina too, and often handily close to the Jemaa el Fna, are the cheapest hotels, with doubles costing around 100dh a night and shared showers and toilets.

If you want to lodge in more tranquil surroundings, it's also worth considering hotels in **Semlalia**, at the northern end of the Ville Nouvelle or, better still, a place out in the **palmery** to the northeast.

All of the top-end hotels and riads, and in fact many of the mid-range places too, take **reservations** online or by email, and even some inexpensive hotels can be booked by email. It's worth booking ahead, especially if you want to stay at one of the mid-range Medina hotels. At certain times of year, most notably around Christmas and Easter, you'll need to have reserved some time in advance, even to stay at one of the cheap hotels.

Jemaa el Fna and the Southern Medina

SEE MAP ON PP.112–113

Dar les Cigognes 108 Rue de Berrima ⊕044 38 27 40, ⊕044 38 47 67, ⊛www.lescigognes.com. A luxury riad run by a Swiss-American couple in two converted Medina houses, done up in traditional fashion around the patio, but with modern decor in the rooms and suites. There's a library, a salon and a terrace where you can see storks nesting on the walls of the royal palace opposite (hence the name, which means "house of the storks"). All rooms are en suite; doubles start at 1500dh.

Hotel Aday 111 Derb Sidi Bouloukat ⊕044 44 19 20. This small budget hotel is well kept, clean and friendly, and pleasantly decorated, with doors and ceilings painted in traditional Marrakshi style. The rooms, grouped around a central patio, are small and don't all have external windows. Shower facilities are shared (5dh), with hot water round the clock. Doubles 80dh; breakfast not included.

Hotel Ali Rue Moulay Ismail ⊕044 44 49 79, ⊕044 44 05 22, ⊕hotelali @hotmail.com. A popular hotel with en-suite rooms, heated in winter and air-conditioned in summer. The hotel is used as an assembly point for various groups heading to the High Atlas, so it's a good source of trekking (and other) information, though it doesn't make a very good job of keeping out hustlers, and at times it has the air of a transport terminal. It also changes money, rents bicycles, has a cybercafé and expedition provisions shop, and can arrange car, minibus or 4x4 rental. There's also a great-value restaurant with all-you-can-eat buffet suppers (see p.56). The rooms vary a lot, so it's worth checking them out before deciding which to take. Book ahead, especially if you are likely to arrive late in the day. Doubles cost 170dh, dorm beds 40dh; both rates include breakfast.

Hotel CTM Jemaa el Fna ⊕044 44 23 25. What's good about this big old hotel is location, location, location – above the former bus station on the Jemaa el Fna. The rooms are of a decent size, if drab. Some rooms have their own shower, but the drawback is the lack of hot water (though you could pop round to one of the hammams nearby). Rooms 28–32 overlook the Jemaa, which means that guests in those rooms can hear the performers day and night; the rooms at the back are much quieter. Breakfast is served on the roof terrace, which also overlooks the square. Doubles from 104dh.

Hotel Essaouira 3 Derb Sidi Bouloukat ⊕044 44 38 05, ⊕044 42 63 23, ⊕hotelessaouira@hotmail.com. One of the most popular cheapies in Marrakesh – with good reason. It's a well-run, safe place, with friendly management, and services like laundry and a baggage deposit (handy if you're going trekking and don't want to carry all your luggage with you). Rooms are small and simple, and there's a rooftop café, where you can have breakfast. Reservations advised. Double rooms from 80dh excluding breakfast.

Hotel Gallia 30 Rue de la Recette ☎044 44 59 13, ℻044 44 48 53, ⓦwww .ilove-marrakesh.com/hotelgallia. In a restored Medina mansion, this little gem is beautifully kept and spotlessly clean. The en-suite rooms are arranged around two tiled courtyards, one of which has a fountain and a palm tree with caged songbirds. There's central heating in winter and air-conditioning in summer. Requires booking by fax, at least a month ahead if possible. Double rooms 410dh.

Hotel La Mamounia Av Bab Jedid ☎044 44 44 09, ℻044 44 49 40, ⓦwww .mamounia.com; toll-free booking: UK ☎0800/181123, Republic of Ireland ☎1800/409063, US and Canada ☎1-800/223 6800, Australia ☎1800/222033, New Zealand ☎0800/441016. Set within its own palatial grounds, this is Marrakesh's most famous hotel, described by former guest Winston Churchill as "the most beautiful place in the world". It is also the most expensive place in town, with all the services you could want – a business centre, a fitness centre, tennis and squash courts, a beauty salon, its own hammam and sauna, a pool of course, five restaurants, five bars and a casino. Decoratively, it is of most interest for the 1920s Art Deco touches by Jacques Majorelle (of Majorelle Garden fame), and their enhancements, in 1986, by the then Moroccan king's favourite designer, André Paccard. Despite the history, the fame and all the trimmings, however, standards of service here do not always match the price, and *La Maison Arabe* (see p.113) is generally better value if you're looking to be pampered, though it can't match the *Mamounia*'s facilities or architectural splendour. Doubles from 3080dh; breakfast not included.

Hotel Medina 1 Derb Sidi Bouloukat ☎044 44 29 97. Located in a street full of good budget hotels, the *Medina* is a perennial favourite among the cheapies, and often full. It's clean, friendly and pretty good value, and the owner – who used to work in Britain as a circus acrobat – speaks good English. There's always hot water in the shared showers (5dh). They have a small roof terrace where you can have breakfast; in summer there's also the option of sleeping on the roof (25dh). Double rooms 100dh excluding breakfast (10dh).

Hotel Sherazade 3 Derb Djama, off Rue Riad Zitoun El Kadim ☎ & ℻044 42 93 05, ⓦwww.hotelsherazade.com. Before riads took off big time, this place was already on the scene, an old merchant's house prettily done up. Besides a lovely roof terrace, the hotel offers a wide variety of well-maintained rooms, some en suite. Run very professionally by a German-Moroccan couple, it's extremely popular with European visitors, so book well ahead. Prices tend to be on the high side compared with the competition (the *Gallia* and the *Jnane Mogador*): doubles start at 430dh, not including breakfast.

Hotel Souria 17 Rue de la Recette ☎044 42 75 45. Deservedly popular family-run hotel. The rooms, set around a pleasant patio, are small and well kept, but the real reason why people like this place is that the women who run it make you feel like a guest in their own home. Hot showers cost 10dh. Double rooms 100dh or 120dh; breakfast not included.

Jnane Mogador Hotel Derb Sidi Bouloukat, by 116 Rue Riad Zitoun El Kadim ☎ & ℻044 42 63 23, ⓦwww .jnanemogador.com. Run by the same management as the *Fssaouira*, this relatively new place is just as homely and is already establishing itself as a favourite place to stay. In a beautifully restored old house, it boasts charming rooms around a lovely fountain patio, and a roof terrace where you can have breakfast, or tea and cake. Great value; doubles 300dh, though the rate doesn't include breakfast.

Riad Kaïss 65 Derb Jedid, off Rue Riad Zitoun El Kadim ☎ & ℻044 44

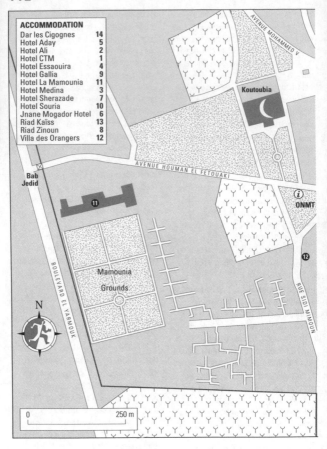

ACCOMMODATION

Dar les Cigognes	14
Hotel Aday	5
Hotel Ali	2
Hotel CTM	1
Hotel Essaouira	4
Hotel Gallia	9
Hotel La Mamounia	11
Hotel Medina	3
Hotel Sherazade	7
Hotel Souria	10
Jnane Mogador Hotel	6
Riad Kaïss	13
Riad Zinoun	8
Villa des Orangers	12

01 41, ⊕www.riadkaiss.com. A luxury riad in a nineteenth-century house done out in quite an interesting contemporary Moroccan style – the light, modern decor seamlessly incorporates traditional features such as windows with stained glass in vivid primary colours. Rooms mostly surround a large open courtyard with orange trees, a fountain and recesses with divans to lounge on. There's also a large, cool salon, and a multi-level roof terrace with pavilions and a pool. Double rooms start at 1465dh.

Riad Zinoun 31 Derb Ben Amrane, off Rue Riad Zitoun El Kadim ☎044 42 67 93, ⊕www.riadzinoun.com. A friendly

little riad, run by a French-Moroccan couple. It isn't the most chic of its kind in the Medina, but it is very pleasant, set around a patio (covered in winter, open in summer) in a nicely refurbished old house. Doubles from €65.

Villa des Orangers 6 Rue Sidi Mimoun, off Place Youssef Ben Tachfine ☎044 38 46 38, ☎044 38 51 23, ⊕www .villadesorangers.com. Officially a hotel, but a riad in the true sense of the term, an old house around a patio garden (two gardens in fact) – with orange trees and a complete overdose of lovely carved stucco. There's a range of rooms and suites, many

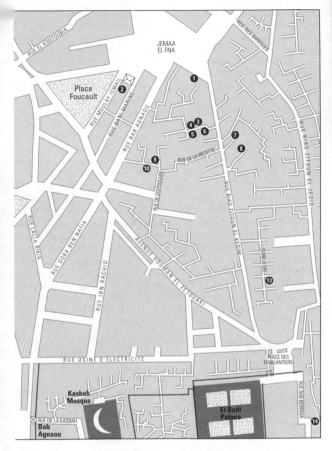

with their own private terrace, a rooftop pool and a spacious salon with a real fire. Doubles from 2900dh, the rate including breakfast and a light lunch.

Northern Medina

SEE MAP ON PP.72–73

Bordj Dar Lamane 11 Derb El Koudia (aka Derb Kabbadj), off Place Ben Salah ℡044 37 85 41, ℻044 33 04 87, ℮suntrek@iam.net.ma. Easy to find from Place Ben Salah (the arch leading to it has a sign painted over it), this is a pleasant

little Moroccan-owned riad in an interesting part of the Medina, far enough from the Jemaa el Fna to avoid the tourist throng, but near enough to be there in 10min when you want to be. There are seven rooms around a patio that's covered in winter, open in summer. The decor is based on traditional features such as painted woodwork, and there's a lovely flower-filled roof terrace. Doubles 1200dh.

La Maison Arabe 1 Derb Assebbe Bab Doukkala, behind the Doukkala mosque ℡044 38 70 10, ℻044 38 72 21, ℮www.lamaisonarabe.com. Though not as famous as the *Mamounia*, this is arguably

Marrakesh's classiest hotel, boasting high standards of service in a gorgeous nine-teenth-century mansion that's been newly restored with fine traditional workmanship. The furnishings are classic Moroccan and sumptuous, as is the food (this was a restaurant before it was a hotel, and it even offers cookery classes). There are two beau-tifully kept patios and a selection of rooms and suites, all with TV, minibar, a/c and heat-ing, some with private terrace and jacuzzi. The premises lack a pool, but the hotel lays on a shuttle bus to take you to its private pool nearby. Doubles from 1724dh, includ-ing breakfast and afternoon tea.

Riad Sindibad 413 Arset Ben Brahim, just inside Bab Yacout ☎044 38 13 10, ⌨www.riad-sindibad.com. Tastefully done up by its French owner, with Moroccan touches, although the feel remains predomi-nantly European. The rooms, set around an intimate patio with a small pool, are com-fortable and en suite, and there's a Jacuzzi on the roof terrace. The location is a bit of a way from the main Medina sights, however. Doubles from €58.

Ville Nouvelle

SEE MAP OPPOSITE

Gueliz

Hotel Agdal 1 Bd Mohammed Zerktouni ☎044 43 36 70, ⌨044 43 12 39. One of the better Guéliz hotels, with a pool, bar and restaurant, and well situated for the restau-rants and cafés around Place Abdelmoumen Ben Ali. Rooms are smallish but have a/c, satellite TV and balcony. Doubles 512dh, not including breakfast.

Hotel des Voyageurs 40 Bd Mohammed Zerktouni ☎044 44 72 18. Has rather an old-fashioned feel, but it's well kept, with spacious rooms and a pleasant little garden. Quiet and peaceful despite being located right at the heart of Guéliz. Doubles from 118dh, not including breakfast.

Hotel Farouk 66 Av Hassan II ☎044 43 19 89, ⌨044 44 05 22, ✉hotelfarouk @hotmail.com. Owned by the same family as the *Ali* (see p.110), this is the top choice

for a budget hotel in the Ville Nouvelle. A slightly eccentric building, with all sorts of branches and extensions, it offers a variety of rooms – have a look at a few before choosing – all with hot showers. Staff are friendly and welcoming, and there's an excellent restaurant. Doubles 150dh.

Hotel Toulousain 44 Rue Tariq Ben Ziad ☎044 43 00 33, ⌨044 43 14 46, ⌨www.geocities.com/hotel_toulousain. Located behind the municipal market, this budget hotel was originally owned by a Frenchman from Toulouse – hence the name. Besides a secure car park and bike rental they have a variety of rooms, some with shower, some with shower and toilet, some with shared facilities. Doubles start at 160dh.

Ibis Moussafir Hotel Av Hassan II/Place de la Gare ☎044 43 59 29 to 32, ⌨044 43 59 36, ⌨www.ibishotel.com. Part of a chain of modern, largely business-oriented hotels. Not the most exciting accommoda-tion in town, but good value, with efficient service, a swimming pool, a restaurant, a bar in the lobby, and good buffet breakfasts included in the rate. Doubles 512dh.

Hivernage

Hotel Atlas Av de France ☎044 33 99 00, ⌨044 43 33 08, ✉atlasmra @iam.net.ma. This four-star establishment is one of the largest and best known of the Hivernage hotels. Outwardly bleak and bar-rack-like, it has comfortable rooms, with minibar and satellite TV, and there are two good restaurants, three bars, a pool, tennis courts, a gym, a sauna and a beauty salon. Most importantly, the hotel is known for its efficient staff and high standards of service. Doubles 1070dh; breakfast not included.

Hotel Imperial Borj 5 Av Echouhada ☎044 44 73 22, ⌨044 44 62 06. A cut above the nearby international chain hotels, this comfortable, modern five-star has decent-sized rooms, a large pool and pleas-ant landscaped gardens. There's a Moroccan and an international restaurant, a piano bar, and lots of marble in the lobby and the bathrooms. Rooms have their own balcony, a/c and heating, satellite TV, mini-bar, and 24hr room service. Doubles 1500dh, excluding breakfast.

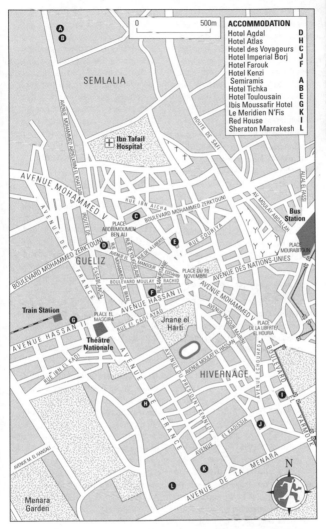

ACCOMMODATION	
Hotel Agdal	D
Hotel Atlas	H
Hotel des Voyageurs	C
Hotel Imperial Borj	J
Hotel Farouk	F
Hotel Kenzi Semiramis	A
Hotel Tichka	B
Hotel Toulousain	E
Ibis Moussafir Hotel	G
Le Meridien N'Fis	K
Red House	I
Sheraton Marrakesh	L

Le Meridien N'Fis Av de France ☎044 33 94 00, ⅁044 33 94 05, ⍟www .lemeridien-hotels.com; toll-free booking: UK ☎0800/028 2840, Ireland ☎1800/409 090, US and Canada ☎1-800/543 4300, Australia ☎1800/622 240, New Zealand ☎0800/454 040. The rooms are nothing special though they do have satellite TV, a/c and heating. The public areas are quite tastefully decorated, however, and the hotel boasts its own pool, hammam, sauna, fitness centre and creche, plus five restaurants. One room is adapted for wheelchair users. Doubles 3700dh, not including breakfast.

Sheraton Marrakesh Av de la Menara ☎044 44 89 98, ⅁044 43 78 43, ⍟www.sheraton.com/marrakech; toll-free booking: UK, Ireland and New Zealand ☎+800/3253 5353, US and Canada ☎1-800/325 3535, Australia ☎1-800/073535.

Basically a package-tour hotel, and feels like it; the rooms, though extremely comfortable with both a/c and heating, are neither huge nor stylishly done out. Besides a large pool and sunbathing area, a jacuzzi and a hammam, the hotel also boasts five restaurants and three bars, including a tapas bar. Wheelchair accessible, with one bedroom adapted for wheelchair users. Doubles from 2030dh, excluding breakfast.

The Red House Bd el Yarmouk opposite the city wall, Hivernage ☎044 43 70 40 or 41, ℻044 44 74 09, ⊛www .theredhouse-marrakech.com. A beautiful nineteenth-century mansion (also called *Dar el Ahmar*) full of fine stucco and *zellij* work downstairs, where the restaurant offers gourmet Moroccan cuisine. Accommodation consists of eight luxurious suites, extremely chic and palatial, though European imperial rather than classic Moroccan. Doubles from 3000dh.

Hotel Kenzi Semiramis Off Av Mohammed Abdelkrim el Kattabi (Route de Casablanca) ☎044 43 13 77, ℻044 44 71 27, ⊛www.kenzi-hotels.com. Part of the Moroccan Kenzi chain which specializes in sports holidays. Though there are facilities for tennis, badminton, *pétanque* and even archery, the main sport here is golf, and the hotel runs a free shuttle bus (except Sun & public holidays) to take guests to the nearby Amelkis golf course. Apart from all this, there are the usual five-star facilities. Doubles 1850dh excluding breakfast; promotional rates often available.

Hotel Tichka Off Mohammed Abdelkrim el Kattabi ☎044 44 87 10, ℻044 44 86 91, ✉tichkasalam@iam.net.ma. Built in 1986, this boasts fine architecture and

decor by Tunisian architect Charles Boccara and the acclaimed American interior designer Bill Willis, including columns in the form of palm trees. Most notable is the use of a super-smooth, beautifully coloured plaster glaze called *tadelakt*, which was traditionally used in hammams to waterproof the walls, and whose use here by Willis made it massively trendy in Moroccan interior design. All rooms have a/c, heating, satellite TV and a minibar, and the hotel has a swimming pool, a health centre and its own hammam. Doubles 1418dh, excluding breakfast.

The palmery

Dar Zemora 72 Rue El Aandalib ☎044 32 82 00, ℻044 61 08 07 61, ⊛www .darzemora.com. A British-owned luxury villa stylishly done out with a mix of traditional and modern features. There's a pleasant garden with a heated pool, a masseur on call, and a view of the Atlas mountains from the roof terrace. All rooms have CD players though no TV. To find it, take the next left (Rue Qortoba) off the Route de Fes after the Circuit de la Palmeraie, then the first right (Rue el Yassamin), fork left after 300m and it's 300m round the bend on the right. Doubles 2300dh.

Hotel Palmeraie Golf Palace Circuit de la Palmeraie, off Route de Casablanca ☎044 30 10 10, ℻044 30 50 50, ⊛www.pgp.co.ma. One of the better five-stars, some way out of town amid wooded countryside, the *Palmeraie Golf Palace* has no fewer than five swimming pools, plus squash and tennis courts, riding stables, and, most importantly, its own eighteen-hole golf course. A favourite with Morocco's late king, Hassan II, the hotel is known for its fine food and high standard of service. Doubles from 4060dh, not including breakfast.

Essentials

Arrival and transport

Marrakesh's **Menara airport** is 4km southwest of town. Arriving before 8am or after about 6pm, you won't always find the BMCE or Banque Populaire kiosks open to change money or traveller's cheques, though the Arrivals hall does have ATMs as well. Taxis will in any case accept euros, and sometimes dollars or sterling, at more or less the equivalent dirham rate, or you can have them call by an ATM en route to your destination.

Petits taxis, which can pick up in front of the airport terminal, will try to overcharge you. It shouldn't cost more than 50dh to reach the Jemaa el Fna or central Guéliz, and it would cost less if you could get the driver to agree to use the meter (he almost certainly won't). Shared *grands taxis*, which also wait in front of the airport building, charge around 60dh for up to six passengers for the trip to the Jemaa el Fna, with similar prices to Guéliz and Hivernage. The #11 bus is supposed to run every half-hour from the stop in front of the airport terminal to the Jemaa el Fna (3.20dh), but it's very erratic.

Transport

The easiest way to get around town is to ride around in one of the beige **petits taxis**. *Petits taxis* take up to three passengers and are equipped with a meter; if the driver doesn't use it, it's because he intends to overcharge you. Most trips around town (*petits taxis* are not allowed beyond the city limits) cost 5–15dh, or 8–20dh at night, when there is a fifty-percent surcharge on the metered fare. If you're a lone passenger, it's standard practice for the driver to pick up one or two additional passengers en route, each of whom will pay the full fare for their journey, as will you. There are *petit taxi* ranks at most major intersections in Guéliz, and in the Medina in the northwest corner of the Jemaa el Fna, at the junction of Avenue Houman el Fetouaki and Rue Oqba Ben Nafia, and at the Place des Ferblantiers end of Avenue Houman el Fetouaki.

Grands taxis

Grands taxis – usually large Mercedes – usually run as shared taxis, taking six passengers (though only designed for four) for a fixed price. You'll probably only want to use a *grand taxi* if you're heading to the **Atlas mountains** or to **Essaouria**.

Grands taxis operate from various ranks around the city, each of which is designated for certain routes. When you arrive at the departure point, ask which vehicle is going to your destination and, unless you want to charter the whole taxi, make clear that you just want individual seats (*une place* for one person, *deux places* for two, etc).

It's possible to **charter** a taxi by paying for all six places. Negotiate the price in advance; if your destination isn't one covered by a regular taxi run, the cost should be roughly equivalent to six fares on a standard journey of that distance.

Bike rental

An alternative for exploring the more scattered sights, such as the Agdal and Menara gardens or the palmery, is a **bicycle** or **moped**. Bicycles can be rented from *Hotel Toulousain* in Guéliz (see p.114), the *Hotel Ali* in the Medina (see p.110), from an outlet in Av el Qadissia behind *Hotel Imperial Borj* in Hivernage, and at 76 Av Mohammed Abdelkrim el Khattabi (Route de Casablanca), opposite Résidence Ezzahia on the edge of Guéliz and Semlalia. The last of these also rents mopeds and motorbikes, as does Marrakesh Motos (aka Chez Jamal Boucetta), 100m up the street at 31 Av Mohammed Abdelkrim el Khattabi (☎044 44 83 59). Expect to pay around 100dh a day for a bicycle, 300dh for a moped.

Grands taxis are fast for journeys out of town, but they are cramped and drivers are prone to speeding and overtaking on blind curves or the brows of hills. They have more than their fair share of crashes in a country where the road accident rate is already high. A lot of accidents involve *grand taxi* drivers falling asleep at the wheel at night, so you may wish to avoid travelling by *grand taxi* after dark.

Calèches

Calèches – horse-drawn cabs – line up near the Koutoubia, the El Badi Palace and some of the fancier hotels. They take up to five people and are not much more expensive than *petits taxis* – though be sure to fix the price in advance, particularly if you want a tour of the town.

Buses

City buses are cheap and efficient. The routes you are most likely to want to use are #1 and #16, which run along Avenue Mohammed V between Guéliz and the Koutoubia. Other handy routes include #6 from the Koutoubia via Bab Ighli to the Agdal gardens, and #11 from the Koutoubia to the Menara gardens and the airport. You board at the rear of the bus and pay the conductor.

Information

The **Moroccan National Tourist Office** (Office National Marocain de Tourisme in French or ONMT for short; ⊛www .tourisme-marocain.com) has offices in several Western cities including London (☎020/7437 0073), New York (☎212/557 2520), Orlando, Florida (☎407/827 5335 or 5337), Montréal (☎514/842 8111) and Sydney (☎02/9922 4999). As well as providing specific information, these offices stock a number of pamphlets on the main Moroccan cities and resorts, and a few items on cultural themes.

The ONMT office in Marrakesh, also called the **Délégation Régional du Tourisme**, is on Place Abdelmoumen Ben Ali in Guéliz (Mon–Fri 8.30am–noon & 2.30–6.30pm, sometimes open Saturdays; ☎044 43 62 39). The staff are generally helpful, and keep a dossier of useful information with listings of hotels, campsites, car-rental firms and other useful contacts. They have a branch office at Place Venus by the Koutoubia (same hours).

A number of Marrakesh **city maps** are available, including Rough Guides' own

Hiring a guide

A local guide can certainly help you find things in the Medina, and a good guide can give some interesting commentary on what you are seeing but, armed with a good map and this book, you won't actually need a guide. That said, **official guides** (150dh for half a day) can be engaged at the ONMT or large hotels. It's illegal to work as an unofficial guide, though unlicensed guides can be found in the Jemaa el Fna, and will appear almost anywhere you're seen looking perplexed.

When hiring a guide, you should tell the guide what you want to see and, with an unlicensed guide, agree a fee very clearly at the outset. Whether official or not, most guides will be wanting to steer you into shops which pay them **commission** on anything you buy (added to your bill, of course). This commission is not small – official guides quite commonly demand as much as fifty percent. You should therefore make it very clear from the start if you do not want to visit any shops or carpet "museums". You may then find that guides lose interest or try to raise their fee.

Marrakesh map, which is printed on tear-proof paper. As for maps easily available locally, the best by a very long chalk is Marocity's "Plan Guide Map", costing around 15dh.

Marrakesh websites

The best website for Marrakesh information is the I Love Marrakech site at ⓦwww.ilovemarrakech.com, with pages on the city's history, the latest weather forecast and Marrakesh news. Add a hyphen to the URL and change the spelling of the city's name, and you reach the much more commercially oriented ⓦwww.ilove-marrakesh.com, where you'll find listings for upmarket hotels, riads and restaurants, plus write-ups and some photos of the main tourist sights. Finally, ⓦwww.elhamra.com has some useful listings of clinics, dental practices, travel agencies and car rental firms, among others, as does ⓦwww .al-bab.com/maroc/trav/marrakesh.htm.

Money

Morocco's unit of currency is the **dirham** (dh), which at the time of writing was selling at approximately 16dh for £1, 9dh for US$1, 11dh for €1. As with all currencies there are fluctuations, but the dirham has roughly held its own against Western currencies over the last few years. The dirham is divided into 100 **centimes** or francs, and you may find prices written or expressed in centimes rather than dirhams. Confusingly, prices are sometimes quoted in **rials**, one rial being five centimes. Coins of 5, 10, 20 and 50 centimes, and 1, 5 and 10 dirhams are in circulation, along with notes of 20, 50, 100 and 200 dirhams. It is illegal to import or export Moroccan dirhams, and they are not usually obtainable abroad.

US and Canadian dollars and pounds sterling (Bank of England – not Scottish or Northern Irish) are easily exchangeable at Marrakesh banks, but **euros** are by far the best hard currency to carry, since they are not only easy to change, but are accepted as cash almost everywhere, at the rate of €1 for 10dh. **Traveller's cheques** are more secure in that you can get them replaced if stolen, but all banks charge 10.75dh per cheque to change them, with the possible exception of the Bank al Maghrib on the Jemaa el Fna, which may agree to change them commission-free.

The main area for **banks** in the Medina is off the south side of the Jemaa el Fna on Rue Moulay Ismail (BMCE and WAFA) and Rue de Bab Agnaou (Banque Populaire, SGMB). In Guéliz, the main area is along Av Mohammed V between Place Abdelmoumen Ben Ali and the market. BMCE's branches in Guéliz (144 Av Mohammed V), the Medina (Rue Moulay Ismail on Place Foucault) and Hivernage (Av de France, opposite *Hotel Atlas*) all have bureaux de change (daily 8.30am–noon & 3–7pm) and ATMs. Outside **banking hours** (which are typically Mon–Thurs 8.15–11.30am & 2.15–4.30pm, Fri 8.15–11.15am & 2.45–4.45pm), the *Hotel Ali* (see p.110) and most upmarket hotels will change traveller's cheques and major hard currencies.

Credit and debit cards

Credit and debit cards belonging to the Visa, Mastercard, Cirrus and Plus networks can be used to withdraw cash from **ATMs**. If you intend to use your plastic, make sure before you leave home that your cards and personal identification numbers (PINs) will work overseas. You can also settle bills in upmarket hotels, restaurants and tourist shops using Mastercard, Visa or American Express cards.

There is usually a weekly limit on cash withdrawals using your card, typically around 5000dh per week, so you may want to carry some cash as a backup or in case your card is lost or stolen (in which event, cancel your card immediately). Note that ATM withdrawals or cash advances obtained with a credit card are treated as loans, with interest accruing

daily from the date of withdrawal. By using plastic in ATMs, you get somewhat better rates than those charged by banks for changing cash. Your card issuer will probably add a foreign transaction fee, worth checking before you travel, but that should still be a good deal lower than the commissions charged by banks for changing cash.

Post, phones and email

Post offices are known as the **PTT** or La Poste. The main **post office** is on Place 16 Novembre, midway down Av Mohammed V in Guéliz (Mon–Fri 8.30am–6.30pm, Sat 8.30am–noon). Here you can buy stamps, send letters and collect poste restante (general delivery) mail. There is a separate office, round the side, for sending parcels. The Medina has a branch post office on the Jemaa el Fna (Mon–Thurs 8.30am–noon & 2.30–6.30pm, Fri 8.30–11.30am & 3–6.30pm; limited services Sat 8.30–11.30am).

The easiest way to make a phone call is to buy a **phonecard** (*télécarte*). Available from most tobacconists and many newsstands in denominations of 18dh, 30dh, 60dh and 99dh, the cards can be used for local or international calls from public phones all over town (there's a whole army of them by the Jemaa el Fna post office). Another way to make a call is to use a **téléboutique** (they're dotted around town – a couple can be found on Rue Bab Agnaou off the Jemaa el Fna), where you make a call and pay for it when you finish. Calling direct from your hotel room is obviously more convenient, but will cost a lot more.

You may well be able to use your **mobile phone** in Marrakesh (US phones need to be GSM to work abroad); check with your phone provider if their roaming agreements cover Morocco. Note that once in Marrakesh you'll pay to receive calls as well as to make them. Prepaid cards from abroad cannot be charged up

or replaced locally, but you can buy a local SIM card (250dh), which could be handy if you need to make plenty of overseas calls or if you expect to receive calls from the Moroccan network. You can buy SIM cards from offices of Maroc Telecom and Méditel.

To **call abroad from Morocco**, dial ☏0044 for the UK, ☏00353 for Ireland, ☏0061 for Australia or ☏0064 for New Zealand, followed by the area code (minus the initial zero) and the number. To call North America, dial ☏001, then the three-digit area code, then the number. When **calling Marrakesh from abroad**, dial the international access code, then country code for Morocco, ☏212, then the number – omitting the initial zero.

If you're **calling within Morocco**, note that Moroccan area codes have in effect been scrapped, and that all Moroccan phones, including mobiles, now have a nine-digit number, all digits of which must be dialled. Marrakesh land-line numbers begin 044, in place of the old 04 area code.

Getting online

There are a growing number of **cybercafés** around town, especially around the Jemaa el Fna; expect to pay around 10dh for an hour online. Note that Internet connections can be very slow as cybercafés often have too many terminals for the bandwidth available, so it's best to turn up during a quiet period, such as first thing in the morning.

Cybercafés around the Jemaa Fna include Cyber Mohamed Yassine, 36 Rue Bab Agnaou (daily 6am–1am); Hana Internet at the southern end of Rue Bab Agnaou (daily 7am–1am); Super Cyber de la Place, in an arcade off Rue Bani Marine by the *Hotel Ichbilia* (daily 9am–11pm) and also within the *Hotel Ali* (see p.110). In Guéliz, cybercafés are surprisingly thin on the ground; try Hey Net in a yard off 100 Rue Mohamed el Bekal (daily 9.30am–10pm).

Opening hours, holidays and festivals

Shops in the Medina tend to open every day from 9am to 6pm, with some closed for lunch (around 1–3pm), especially on a Friday. In the Ville Nouvelle, shops are much more likely to close for lunch, but tend to stay open later, until 7 or 8pm, and to close on Sundays. Offices are usually open Monday to Thursday 8.30am–noon and 2.30–6.30pm; on Friday their hours are typically 8.30am–11.30am and 3–6.30pm. Restaurants generally open between noon and 3pm, and again from 7pm to 11pm; only the cheaper places tend to open through the afternoon.

All these opening hours change completely during the holy month of **Ramadan** (which starts around Oct 5 in 2005, Sept 24 in 2006, and Sept 13 in 2007), when Muslims fast from daybreak to nightfall. At this time, shops, offices and banks stay open through the middle of the day and close at 3 or 4pm to allow staff to go home to break the fast. Restaurants may close completely during Ramadan, or open after dusk only, though a couple of places on the Jemaa el Fna will be open through the day to serve tourists.

The biggest religious festivals are **Aid el Kebir**, celebrating the prophet Abraham's willingness to sacrifice his son to God; and **Aid es Seghir**, celebrating the end of Ramadan. For both these festivals, shops and offices will be closed for two days. The main secular holiday is the

Public holidays in Morocco

Islamic religious holidays occur according to the Muslim lunar calendar, in which months begin when the new moon is sighted. Dates for these holidays in the Western (Gregorian) calendar are impossible to predict exactly, so they may vary by a day or two from the approximate dates given here. The main ones (each involving two days' public holiday) are:

Aid el Kebir	Around Jan 21 in 2005, Jan 11 & Dec 31 in 2006, Dec 20 in 2007
Aid es Seghir	Around Nov 3 in 2005, Oct 28 in 2006, Oct 13 in 2007

Other public holidays are:

New Year's Day	Jan 1	**Allegiance Day**	Aug 14
Anniversary of Independence Manifesto	Jan 11	**King's Birthday and Youth Day**	Aug 21
Labour Day	May 1	**Anniversary of the Green March**	Nov 6
Fête Nationale	May 23	**Independence Day**	Nov 18
Feast of the Throne	July 30		

Feast of the Throne, celebrating the king's accession.

Marrakesh has three important annual events of its own. The **Marrakesh Marathon** (Wwww.marathon-marrakech .com) takes place on the third or fourth Sunday in January, the circuit taking 5000 competitors through the palmery and around the Medina. In June, the El Badi Palace and other venues in the city host a two-week **Festival National des Art Populaires** featuring performances by musicians and dancers from all over Morocco and beyond, plus spectacular displays of horsemanship each evening at Bab Jedid west of the Koutoubia. October sees the **Marrakesh Film Festival**, in which the featured movies are shown at cinemas across town, and on large screens in the El Badi Palace and the Jemaa el Fna.

Cultural hints

Don't assume that everyone who approaches you on the street in Marrakesh is a **hustler**. Too many visitors do, and end up making little contact with some of the most hospitable people in the world. In any case, in recent years the hustlers have largely been cleared off the streets by police action. Those that remain include a few dope dealers and confidence tricksters, but most will simply be aiming to have you engage them as unofficial guides (see box, p.120).

It's often said that women are second-class citizens in Morocco and other Islamic countries, but Muslim women are usually keen to point out that this is a misinterpretation of women's position in Muslim society. In some ways the sexes are not as unequal as they seem: men traditionally rule in the street, which is their domain, the women's being the home.

Some **women travellers** experience constant sexual harassment, while others have little or no trouble. The obvious strategies for getting rid of unwanted attention are the same as you would use at home: appear confident and assured and you'll avoid a lot of trouble. Moroccan women are traditionally coy and aloof. You should also avoid physical contact with Moroccan men, even in a manner that would not be considered sexual at home, since it could easily be misunderstood. On the other hand, If a Moroccan man touches you he has definitely crossed the line, and you should not be afraid to **make a scene**. Shouting *shooma!* ("shame on you!") is likely to result in bystanders intervening on your behalf.

Visitors of both sexes should be aware of the importance of **appropriate dress**. It is true that in cities some Moroccan women wear short-sleeved tops and knee-length skirts (and may suffer more harassment as a result), and men do wear sleeveless T-shirts and above-the-knee shorts. However, the Muslim idea of modest dress requires women to be covered from wrist to ankle, and men from above the elbow to below the knee. The best guide is to note how most Moroccans dress, not how other tourists choose to. For women, wearing long sleeves, long skirts and baggy rather than tight clothes will give an impression of respectability. Wearing a headscarf to cover your hair and ears gives this impression even more.

Photography needs to be undertaken with care. If you are obviously taking a photograph of someone, ask their permission. In places much frequented by tourists, you'll often find that local people will demand money for the privilege, especially in the Jemaa el Fna, where bystanders who spot you taking a photograph in which they might feature may be aggressive in asking for money. On a positive note, taking a photograph of someone you've struck up a friendship with and sending it on to them, or exchanging photographs, is often greatly appreciated.

If you're invited to a home, you normally take your **shoes** off before entering the reception rooms – follow your host's lead. It is customary to take a gift: sweet pastries or tea and sugar are always acceptable. If you're **dining**, handle food with your **right hand**; the left is used for "unclean" functions such as wiping your bottom or washing your feet.

During **Ramadan**, when most people are committed to fasting, it's a good idea to be discreet about eating, drinking and smoking during the daytime, and best if possible to confine those activities to your hotel room. Finally, note that in Morocco non-Muslims are excluded from **mosques**, which are regarded as set aside specifically for prayer. Non-Muslims are also excluded from *zaouias*, saints' tombs and some cemeteries.

Directory

Airlines British Airways c/o Menara Tours, 41 Rue de Yougoslavie (by ONMT) ☎044 44 66 54; Royal Air Maroc, 197 Av Mohammed V ☎044 42 55 00 or 01; Regional Air Lines, Menara airport ☎044 43 57 36.

Airport information On ☎044 44 78 65.

American Express c/o Voyages Schwartz, Immeuble Moutaouakil, 1 Rue Mauritanie, Guéliz ☎044 43 33 21, ☎044 43 33 21 (Mon–Fri 9am–12.30pm & 3–6.30pm, Sat 9am–12.30pm).

Bus stations Long-distance buses run by the state-owned CTM (Compagnie des Transports du Maroc; ☻www.ctm.co.ma) operate from their office on Boulevard Mohammed Zerktouni. Most privately run buses use the *gare routière*, Marrakesh's main bus station, which is just outside the walls of the Medina by Bab Doukkala. It's served by buses #3, #8, #10, #14 or #16 from the Koutoubia. Buses to Essaouira, Agadir and the Western Sahara run by Supratours, in conjunction with the train company ONCF, run from in front of the train station (see p.127). Note that on long-distance bus journeys you're expected to tip the porters who load your baggage onto buses (5dh – except on CTM, which has charges by weight).

Cookery courses The *Maison Arabe* (see p.113) offers workshops in Moroccan cooking to guests. It's also possible to learn Moroccan cooking with the Rhode School of Cuisine (☻www.rhodeschoolofcuisine .com), who offer week-long courses from $2000 per person, including villa accommodation in the palmery and meals on site.

Cinemas In Guéliz, the Colisée, alongside the *Café Le Siroua* on Bd Mohammed Zerktouni, is one of the best in town. It shows mainstream releases and has recently enjoyed a face-lift. In the Medina, the Cinéma Mabrouka on Rue Bab Agnaou and the Cinéma Eden, off Rue Riad Zitoun el Jedid, are more downmarket, and usually show a Bollywood/kung fu double bill – known locally as "*l'histoire et la géographie*".

Clinics Dr Abdelmajid Ben Tbib, 171 Av Mohammed V (☎044 43 10 30) is recommended and speaks English. Dr Frédéric Reitzer, Immeuble Moulay Youssef, Rue de la Liberté, Guéliz (☎044 43 95 62) is used by the French consulate and speaks some English. Two private clinics that have high standards and are accustomed to settling bills with insurance companies are Clinique al Koutoubia, Rue de Paris, Hivernage (☎044 43 85 85); Clinique Yassine, 12 Rue Ibn Toumert (☎044 43 33 23); and Polyclinque du Sud, at the corner of Rue Yougoslavie and Rue Ibn Aïcha, Guéliz (☎044 44 79 99). There's an emergency call-out service, SOS Médecins (☎044 40 40 40), which charges 400dh per consultation.

Consulates France, 1 Rue Ibn Khaldoun ☎044 38 82 00; UK, Honorary Consul at Residence Taib, 55 Boulevard Zerktouni ☎044 43 50 95 (in emergencies only); Sweden, Immeuble As-Saad, corner of Rue Moulay Ali and Rue de Yougoslavie ☎044 44 82 51.

Customs allowances One litre of wine or spirits and 200 cigarettes.

Dentist Dr Bennani, on the first floor of 112 Av Mohammed V (☎044 44 91 36), opposite the ONMT office in Guéliz, is recommended and speaks some English.

Electricity Most buildings are on 220V but you may still find a 110V supply in some places, and sometimes even both in the same building. Plug sockets are the same as those in France, with two round pins, so plugs with square or flat pins will need an adapter, best brought from home, as you won't find one easily in Marrakesh.

Emergencies Fire ☎15; police ☎19. The tourist police (*brigade touristique*; ☎044 38 46 01), set up especially to help tourists, are based at the northern end of Rue Sidi Mimoun, just south of the Koutoubia.

Gay Marrakesh Although sexual segregation makes it relatively widespread, gay sex between men is illegal in Morocco, and attitudes to it are different from those in the West. A Moroccan who takes the dominant role in gay intercourse may well not consider himself to be indulging in a homosexual act, and no Moroccan man will declare himself gay – which has connotations of femininity and weakness. The idea of being a passive partner is virtually taboo. As for meeting places in Marrakesh, a certain amount of cruising goes on in the crowds of the Jemaa el Fna in the evening, and there's a gay presence at the *Diamant Noir* nightclub (see p.95). The *Café de la Renaissance* on Place Abdelmoumen Ben Ali in Guéliz used to be another venue for gay men to meet, but this was closed for renovation at the time of writing. There is no public perception of lesbianism, and opportunities for Western women to make contact with Moroccan lesbians are pretty much nil.

Golf There are three eighteen-hole golf courses in Marrakesh: the Marrakesh Royal Golf Club (☎044 40 98 28, ℻044 40 00 84), 10km out of town on the old Ouarzazate road, once played on by Churchill and Eisenhower; the Palmeraie Golf Club (☎044 30 10 10, ℻044 30 20 20), built, as the name suggests, in Youssef Ben Tachfine's palmery, off the Route de Casablanca, northeast of town; and the Amelkis Golf Club, 12km out on the Route de Ouarzazate (☎044 40 44 14, ℻044 40 44 15). All courses are open to non-members, with green fees at around 450dh per day.

Hammams A hammam is a Turkish-style steam bath (expect to pay around 10dh), with a succession of rooms from cool to hot, and endless supplies of hot and cold water, which you fetch in buckets. The usual procedure is to find a piece of floor space in the hot room, surround it with as many buckets of water as you feel you

need, and lie in the heat to sweat out the dirt from your pores before scrubbing it off. A plastic bowl is useful for scooping the water from the buckets to wash with. You can also order a massage, in which you will be allowed to sweat, pulled about a bit to relax your muscles, and then rigorously scrubbed with a rough flannel glove (*kiis*). For many Moroccan women, the hammam is a social gathering place, in which women tourists are made very welcome too. Indeed, hammams turn out to be a highlight for many women travellers, and an excellent way to make contact with Moroccan women. There are quite a lot of hammams in the Medina; the three closest to, and all south of, the Jemaa el Fna are Hammam Polo on Rue de la Recette; one on the same street as *Hôtel Afriquia*, and one at the northern end of Rue Riad Zitoun El Kadim. All three are open throughout the day, with separate entrances for men and women. North of the Jemaa el Fna, there's Hammam Dar el Bacha at 20 Rue Fatima Zohra (daily: noon–7pm women only; at other times men only). Note that nudity is taboo, so you should keep your underwear on (bring a dry change) or wear a swimming costume, and change with a towel around you.

Laundry Most hotels offer a laundry service – in the cheapest places the chambermaid will usually do it herself. Failing that, try the Blanchisserie Oasis, 44 Rue Tarik Ibn Zaid, behind the municipal market in Guéliz (☎044 43 45 78), or Blanchisserie du Sud, 10 Rue Bab Agnaou, near the Jemaa el Fna (☎044 44 33 31).

Newspapers The most reliable newsagent for American and British newspapers is outside the ONMT office on Av Mohammed V in Guéliz, though you'll find *USA Today*, the *International Herald Tribune* and various British dailies on sale at stalls elsewhere, especially around the south side of Jemaa el Fna.

Pharmacies There are several along Av Mohammed V, including a good one, the Pharmacie de la Liberté, just off Place de la Liberté. In the Medina, try Pharmacie de la Place and Pharmacie du Progrés on Rue Bab Agnaou just off the Jemaa el Fna. There's an all-night pharmacy by the Commissariat de Police on the Jemaa el Fna and another on Rue Khalid Ben Oualid near the fire station in Guéliz. Other all-night and weekend outlets are listed in pharmacy windows and in local newspapers such as *Le Message de Marrakech*.

Swimming pools Many hotels (but, alas, not the *Mamounia*) allow non residents to use their pools if you have a meal, or for a fee. Useful places to try are the *Grand Hotel Tazi* south of Jemaa el Fna and the *Hotel Yasmine* on Bd el Yarmouk, both charging 50dh per day. Municipal pools, open in July and August only, are the preserve of male youth, which means women will not find them comfortable places to swim. There's a large municipal pool on Rue Abou el Abbes Sebti (the first main road to the left off Av Mohammed V as you walk past the Koutoubia towards Guéliz).

Time Morocco is on Greenwich Mean Time all year, the same time zone as Britain and Ireland in winter, an hour behind in summer. It's five hours ahead of the US east coast (EST) and eight ahead of the west coast (PST), an hour less in summer; and it's eight hours behind western Australia, ten hours behind eastern Australia, and twelve hours behind New Zealand, an hour more in those places if daylight saving time is in operation.

Tipping You're expected to tip waiters in cafés (1dh per person) and restaurants (5dh or so).

Trains Marrakesh's train station (☏044 44 65 69) is on Avenue Hassan II, on the edge of Guéliz. You could walk here from the centre of Guéliz in about fifteen minutes. Buses #3, #8, #10 and #14 run to the station from Place Foucault by the Jemaa el Fna.

Vegetarian food Vegetarianism used to be pretty much unheard of in Morocco, but awareness is slowly increasing, especially in places used to dealing with tourists. Meat stock and animal fat are widely used in cooking, even in dishes that do not contain meat as such, and you may be best off just turning a blind eye to this. Some restaurants around the Jemaa el Fna that are popular with tourists do offer vegetarian versions of couscous and tajine. Otherwise, the cheaper restaurants serve omelettes, salads and sometimes *bisara* (pea soup), with fancier restaurants offering good salads and sometimes pizza. To tell people you're vegetarian, you could try *ana nabaati* in Arabic, or *je suis vegetarien/vegetarienne* in French. To reinforce the point, you could perhaps add *la akulu lehoum* (*wala hout*) in Arabic, or *je ne mange aucune sorte de viande* (*ou poisson*), both of which mean "I don't eat any kind of meat (or fish)".

Language

Language

Language

The most important language in Marrakesh is **Moroccan Arabic**, as different from the Arabic of the Middle East as Jamaican patois is from British or American English. For many Marrakshis, Arabic is in fact a second language, their first being **Tashelhait** (also called Chleuh), the indigenous Berber language spoken here since before the Arab invasion. Most people in Marrakesh also speak **French**, which is handy if you ever learned that at school.

Even if you learn no other Arabic phrases, it's useful to know the all-purpose greeting, *assalaam aleikum* ("peace to you"); the reply is *waaleikum salaam* ("and to you peace"). When speaking of anything in the future, Moroccans usually say *insha'allah* ("God willing"), and when talking of any kind of good fortune, they say *alhamdulillah* ("praise be to God"). It is normal to respond to these expressions by repeating them. Typically Moroccan phrases that you'll probably hear a lot include *makaynsh mooshkil* ("no problem") and *kif-kif* or *p'hal-p'hal* ("same thing", often meaning "I don't mind either" when someone needs to make a choice). If you really want to impress people, you could try some Tashelhait: "hello" is *manzakin* (with the stress on the second syllable) and "thank you" is *tanmeert*.

Useful terms and phrases

Here is some basic Arabic and French vocabulary for everyday communication. You may find it handy to supplement this list with a phrasebook, such as the *Rough Guide French Dictionary Phrasebook*.

Both Arabic and French have genders, even for inanimate objects, and the word ending varies slightly according to the gender. In the Arabic transliteration, we've used **kh** to represent the sound of ch in "loch", and **gh** to represent a gargling sound similar to a French "r". A **q** represents a "k" pronounced in the back of the throat rather than a "kw", and **j** is like the "zh" in Dr Zhivago; **r** should be trilled, as in Spanish. In Arabic words of more than one syllable, the stressed syllable is shown in bold.

English	Arabic	French
Basics and everyday phrases		
yes	**eych, naa**m	oui
no	la	non
I	ena	moi
you	**ent**a	vous
he	**hoo**wa	lui
she	**hee**ya	elle
we	**neh**noo	nous
they	hoom	ils/elles
(very) good	me**zyen** (**bzef**)	(très) bon
big	ke**beer**	grand
small	se**gheer**	petit
old	ke**deem**	vieux
new	je**deed**	nouveaux
a little	**shwee**ya	un peu
a lot	bzef	beaucoup
open	mah**lul**	ouvert
closed	mas**dud**	fermé
hello/how's it going?	le **bes**?	ça va?

LANGUAGE

Useful terms and phrases

good morning	sbah l'kheer	bonjour
good evening	msa l'kheer	bon soir
good night	leila saeeda	bonne nuit
goodbye	biselama	au revoir
who...?	shkoon...?	qui...?
when...?	imta...?	quand...?
why...?	alash...?	pourquoi...?
how...?	kifesh...?	comment...?
which/ what...?	shnoo...?	quel...?
is there...	kayn...	est-ce qu'il y a...
do you have...	andak... /kayn...	avez-vous...
please	afak/minfadlak to a man or afik/minfadlik to a woman	s'il vous plaît
thank you	shukran	merci
ok/agreed	wakha	d'accord
that's enough/ that's all	safee	suffit
excuse me	ismahlee	excusez-moi
sorry	samakhanee	pardon
let's go	nimsheeyoo	on y va
go away	imshee	va t'en
I don't understand	mafahemsh	je ne comprends pas
do you (m/f) speak English?	takelem/ takelmna ingleesi?	parlez-vous anglais?

Directions

where's...	fayn...	où est...
the airport	el matar	l'aeroport
the train station	mahattat el tren	la gare de train
bus station	mahattat el car	la gare routière
bank	bank	banque
hospital	mostashfa	hôpital
near/far (from here)	qurayab/baeed (min huna)	près/loin (d'ici)
left	liseer	à gauche
right	limeen	à droit
straight ahead	neeshan	tout droit
here	hna	ici
there	temma	là

Accommodation

hotel	funduq	hôtel
do you have a room?	kayn beet?	avez-vous une chambre?
two beds	jooj tlik	deux lits
one big bed	wahad tlik kebir	un grand lit
shower	doosh	douche
hot water	maa skhoona	eau chaud
can I see?	mumkin ashoofha?	je peux le voir?
key	sarut	clé

Shopping

I (don't) want...	ena (mish) bgheet...	je (ne) veux (pas)...
how much (money)?	shahal (flooss)?	combien (d'argent)?
(that's) expensive	(hada) ghalee	(c'est) cher

Numbers

0	sifr	zéro
1	wahad	un
2	jooj	deux
3	tlata	trois
4	arbaa	quatre
5	khamsa	cinq
6	sitta	six
7	sebaa	sept
8	temanya	huit
9	tisaoud	neuf
10	ashra	dix
11	hadashar	onze
12	etnashar	douze
13	talatashar	treize
14	arbatashar	quatorze
15	khamstashar	quinze
16	sittashar	seize
17	sebatashar	dix-sept
18	tamantashar	dix-huit
19	tisatashar	dix-neuf
20	ashreen	vingt
21	wahad wa ashreen	vingt-et-un
22	jooj wa ashreen	vingt-deux
30	talateen	trente
40	arbaeen	quarante
50	khamseen	cinqante
60	sitteen	soixante
70	sabaeen	soixante-dix
80	tamaneen	quatre vingts

90	tisaeen	quatre-vingt-dix
100	mia	cent
121	mia wa wahad wa ashreen	cent vingt-et-un
200	miateen	deux cents
300	tolta mia	trois cents
1000	alf	mille
a half	nuss	demi
a quarter	roba	quart

Days and times

Monday	nahar el itneen	lundi
Tuesday	nahar et telat	mardi
Wednesday	nahar el arbaa	mercredi
Thursday	nahar el khemis	jeudi
Friday	nahar el jemaa	vendredi
Saturday	nahar es sabt	samedi
Sunday	nahar el had	dimanche
yesterday	imbarih	hier
today	el yoom	aujourd'hui
tomorrow	gheda	demain
what time is it?	shahal fisa'a?	quelle heure est-il?
one o'clock	sa'a wahda	une heure
2.15	jooj wa roba	deux heures et quart
3.30	tlata wa nuss	trois heures et demi
4.45	arbaa ila roba	quatre heures moins quart

Food and drink basics

restaurant	mataam	restaurant
breakfast	iftar	petit déjeuner
egg	beyd	ouef
butter	zibda	beurre
jam	marmalad	confiture
cheese	jibna	fromage
yoghurt	rayeb	yaourt
salad	salata	salade
olives	zitoun	olives
bread	khobz	pain
salt	melha	sel
pepper	haroor	piment
(without)	(bilesh)	(sans)
sugar	sukkar	sucre

the bill	el hisab	l'addition
fork	forsheta	fourchette
knife	moos	couteau
spoon	malka	cuillère
plate	tabseel	assiete

Meat, poultry and fish

meat	lahem	viande
beef	baqri	boeuf
chicken	djaj	poulet
lamb	houli	mouton
liver	kibda	foie
pigeon	hamam	pigeon
fish	hout	poisson
prawns	qambri	crevettes

Vegetables

vegetables	khadrawat	légumes
artichoke	qoq	artichaut
aubergine	badinjan	aubergine
beans	loobia	haricots
onions	basal	oignons
potatoes	batata	potates
tomatoes	mateesha	tomates

Fruits and nuts

almonds	looz	amandes
apple	tufah	pomme
banana	banan	banane
dates	tmer	dattes
grapes	anab	raisins
lemon	limoon	limon
melon	battikh	melon
orange	limoon	orange
prickly pear (cactus fruit)	hendiya	figues de Barbarie
watermelon	dellah	pastèque

Beverages

water	maa	de l'eau
mineral water	Sidi Ali/Sidi Harazom (brand names)	eau minérale
ice	jeleedi	glace
ice cream	glace	glace
milk	haleeb	lait
coffee	qahwa	café
coffee with a little milk	nuss nuss	café cassé
coffee with plenty of milk	qahwa bi haleeb	café au lait/ café crème

tea (with mint/ wormwood)	atay (bi nana/ sheeba)	thé (à la menthe/ à l'absinthe)
juice	aseer	jus
beer	birra	bière
wine	sharab	vin
almond milk (crushed almonds steeped in water)	aseer looz	jus d'amande
apple milkshake	aseer tufah	jus de pomme
banana milkshake	aseer banan	jus des bananes
orange juice	aseer limoon	jus d'orange
mixed fruit milkshake	–	jus panache

Common dishes and foods

bisara	thick pea soup, usually served with olive oil and cumin
chakchouka	a vegetable stew not unlike ratatouille, though sometimes containing meat or eggs
couscous aux sept legumes	seven-vegetable couscous (sometimes vegetarian, though often made with meat stock)
harira	bean soup, usually also containing pasta and meat
kefta	minced meat (usually lamb)
loobia	bean stew
mechoui	roast lamb
merguez	small, spicy dark red sausages – typically lamb, though sometimes of beef – usually grilled over charcoal

pastilla	sweet pigeon or chicken pie with cinnamon and filo pastry, a speciality of Fes
(pommes) frites	French fries
salade Marocaine	salad of tomato and cucumber, finely chopped
tajine	a Moroccan casserole cooked over charcoal in a thick ceramic bowl (which is what the word really refers to) with a conical lid
tajine aux olives et citron	tajine of chicken with olive and preserved lemon
tanjia	a Marrakshi speciality, jugged beef – the term in fact refers to the jug

Breads and pastries

briouats/ doits de Fatima	sweet filo pastry with a savoury filling, a bit like a miniature pastilla
briouats au miel	sweet filo pastry envelopes filed with nuts and honey
cornes de gazelles (Fr.)/ kab l-ghazl (Ar.)	marzipan-filled, banana-shaped pastry horns
harsha	flat, leavened griddle bread with a gritty crust, served at cafés for breakast
millefeuille	custard slice
msammen	flat griddle bread made from dough sprinkled with oil, rolled out and folded over several times, rather like an Indian paratha

Glossary

Alaouites (also spelt **Alawites**) The dynasty to which Morocco's present king, Mohammed VI, belongs, and which first came to power in 1668. The Alaouites trace their ancestry back to the Prophet Mohammed.

Almohads A religious movement of Berbers based at Tinmal in the Atlas. They took Marrakesh in 1147 and made it the capital of an empire stretching from Spain to Tunisia.

Almoravids A fundamentalist movement of Mauritanian Berber nomads who conquered Marrakesh in 1062 and held it until 1147.

argan A tree that grows only in the south of Morocco, bearing a fruit whose pip yields a sweet and much prized oil.

bab Gate or door.

ben Son of, eg "Ben Youssef" meaning "the son of Youssef".

Berbers The indigenous population of Morocco prior to the seventh-century Arab invasion. Even today, Marrakesh is as much a Berber city as an Arab one, and the regional Berber language, Tashelhait, is widely spoken.

calèche Horse-drawn carriage.

dar Mansion or palace.

derb Alley.

Fes (also spelt **Fez** in English, **Fès** in French) Marrakesh's long-time rival as Morocco's cultural and political capital, and still considered its main spiritual, musical and culinary centre.

fondouk Caravanserai; an inn for travelling merchants.

ginbri Skin-covered two- or three-string lutes, originally from West Africa, and a favourite Gnaoua instrument.

Gnaoua Member of a Sufi (Muslim mystic) fraternity of musicians, originally from West Africa (the word *gnaoua* comes from the same root as Guinea).

hammam In principle just a bath or bathroom, but it refers in particular to a traditional steam bath with a hotroom, much the same as a Turkish bath.

jellaba A long garment with sleeves and a hood.

kasbah A fortified area within a city, often the citadel. In the case of Marrakesh, it's a walled residential district in the southwest of the Medina.

kissaria Covered market, especially the textile market at the heart of the Medina's souks.

koubba A dome, but also used for the domed building the constructed over the tomb of a saint.

marabout Itinerant holy man or woman, often credited with divine powers (to exorcize demons, for example).

medersa Religious school where pupils are taught to read, write and recite the Koran.

Merenids A Berber tribe from eastern Morocco who took power in Fes in 1248, conquered Marrakesh in 1269, and remained in power until 1465.

mihrab The niche in a mosque indicating the direction of Mecca, and thus of prayer.

minbar The wooden pulpit in a mosque.

minzah A pavilion in a park.

moulay A descendant of the Prophet Mohammed.

moussem Annual local festival celebrating a saint's day.

oued Wadi; a seasonal watercourse.

pisé Clay and straw used for construction of walls and buildings.

raï Originally from Algeria, the most popular type of pop music in Morocco, mainly in the form of love songs.

riad A patio garden, and by extension a house with a patio garden.

Saadians A dynasty of descendants of the Prophet, from the Souss Valley in Morocco's far south. They took Marrakesh in 1521, made it their capital, and ruled until 1668.

sidi Respectful term used to address a man; also used to refer to a Muslim saint.

souk Market, in particular a part of the Medina where shops or workshops of one type are gathered.

Sufi Muslim mystic, belonging to a brotherhood (there are several brotherhoods in Morocco).

thuya (also spelt **thuja**; **arar** in Arabic) An aromatic mahogany-like hardwood from a local coniferous tree.

Yacoub el Mansour The third Almohad sultan (ruled 1184–99), whose reign arguably marked Marrakesh's golden age.

Youssef Ben Tachfine Marrakesh's founder, the first Almoravid sultan, buried to the south of the Koutoubia mosque.

zaouia The sanctuary established around the tomb of a marabout, often the base of a Sufi (mystic) religious brotherhood.

zellij Tilework, especially a form in which small pieces of ceramic tiles are cut into shapes that fit into a geometrical mosaic design, usually based on a star with a specific number of points.

ROUGH GUIDES
TRAVEL SERIES

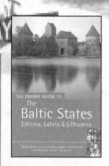

THE ROUGH GUIDE TO
The Baltic States
Estonia, Latvia & Lithuania

THE ROUGH GUIDE TO
China

THE ROUGH GUIDE TO
Florida

THE ROUGH GUIDE TO
South America

THE ROUGH GUIDE TO
Sweden

THE ROUGH GUIDE TO
USA

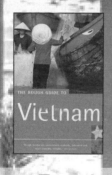

THE ROUGH GUIDE TO
Vietnam

THE ROUGH GUIDE TO
Vancouver

THE ROUGH GUIDE TO
The Philippines

**Travel guides to more than
250 destinations
from Alaska to Zimbabwe**

smooth travel

ROUGH GUIDES TRAVEL...

Rough Guides are available from good bookstores worldwide. New titles are published every month. Check www.roughguides.com for the latest news.

...MUSIC & REFERENCE

Zanzibar
Zimbabwe

Travel Theme guides

First-Time Around the World
First-Time Asia
First-Time Europe
First-Time Latin America
Gay & Lesbian Australia
Skiing & Snowboarding in North America
Travel Online
Travel Health
Walks in London & SE England
Women Travel

Restaurant guides

French Hotels & Restaurants
London
New York
San Francisco

Maps

Algarve
Amsterdam
Andalucia & Costa del Sol
Argentina
Athens
Australia
Baja California
Barcelona
Boston
Brittany
Brussels
Chicago
Crete
Croatia
Cuba
Cyprus
Czech Republic

Dominican Republic
Dublin
Egypt
Florence & Siena
Frankfurt
Greece
Guatemala & Belize
Iceland
Ireland
Lisbon
London
Los Angeles
Mexico
Miami & Key West
Morocco
New York City
New Zealand
Northern Spain
Paris
Portugal
Prague
Rome
San Francisco
Sicily
South Africa
Sri Lanka
Tenerife
Thailand
Toronto
Trinidad & Tobago
Tuscany
Venice
Washington DC
Yucatán Peninsula

Dictionary Phrasebooks

Czech
Dutch
Egyptian Arabic
European
French
German
Greek
Hindi & Urdu
Hungarian
Indonesian

Italian
Japanese
Mandarin Chinese
Mexican Spanish
Polish
Portuguese
Russian
Spanish
Swahili
Thai
Turkish
Vietnamese

Music Guides

The Beatles
Bob Dylan
Cult Pop
Classical Music
Country Music
Cuban Music
Drum'n'bass
Elvis
Hip Hop
House
Irish Music
Jazz
Music USA
Opera
Reggae
Rock
Techno
World Music (2 vols)

100 Essential CDs series

Country
Latin
Opera
Rock
Soul
World Music

History Guides

China
Egypt
England
France

Greece
India
Ireland
Islam
Italy
Spain
USA

Reference Guides

Books for Teenagers
Children's Books 0–5
Children's Books 5–11
Cult Fiction
Cult Football
Cult Movies
Cult TV
Digital Stuff
Ethical Shopping
Formula 1
iPods & iTunes
The Internet
Internet Radio
James Bond
Kids' Movies
Lord of the Rings
Man Utd
Muhammad Ali
PCs & Windows
Pregnancy & Birth
Shakespeare
Superheroes
Travel Health
Travel Online
Unexplained Phenomena
The Universe
Videogaming
Weather
Website Directory

ROUGH GUIDES

Also! More than 120 Rough Guide music CDs are available from all good book and record stores. Listen in at www.worldmusic.net

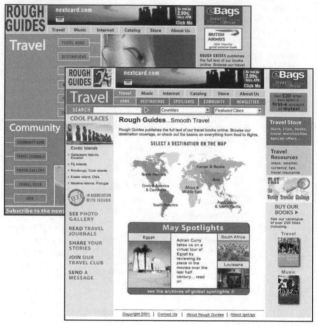

ROUGH GUIDE MAPS

Printed on waterproof and rip-proof Polyart™ paper, offering an unbeatable combination of practicality, clarity of design and amazing value.

CITY MAPS
Amsterdam · Athens · Barcelona · Berlin · Boston · Chicago
Brussels · Dublin · Florence & Siena · Frankfurt · London
Lisbon · Los Angeles · Madrid · Marrakesh · Miami
New York · Paris · Prague · Rome · San Francisco · Toronto
Venice · Washington DC and more...

COUNTRY & REGIONAL MAPS
Algarve · Andalucía · Argentina · Australia · Baja California
Brittany · Crete · Croatia · Cuba · Cyprus · Czech Republic
Dominican Republic · Dubai & UAE Egypt · Greece
Guatemala & Belize · Hong Kong · Iceland · Ireland · Kenya
Mexico · Morocco · New Zealand · Northern Spain · Peru
Portugal · Sicily · South Africa · South India · Sri Lanka
Tenerife · Thailand · Trinidad & Tobago · Tuscany
Yucatán Peninsula and more...

The ROUGH GUIDE to
Walks in London and Southeast England

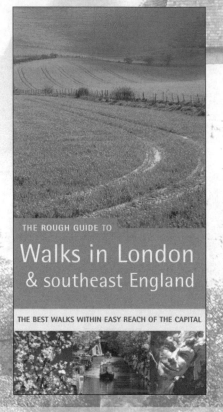

THE ROUGH GUIDE TO

Walks in London
& southeast England

THE BEST WALKS WITHIN EASY REACH OF THE CAPITAL

From picturesque towpath and woodland walks in the heart of the city to get-away-from-it-all hikes through the Chilterns and South Downs – the best walks within easy reach of the capital.

Available from your local bookstore
or online at www.roughguides.com

ISBN 1-85828-938-6, 288pp

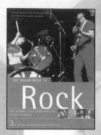

Index and small print

SMALL PRINT

A Rough Guide to Rough Guides

Marrakesh DIRECTIONS is published by Rough Guides. The first *Rough Guide to Greece*, published in 1982, was a student scheme that became a publishing phenomenon. The immediate success of the book – with numerous reprints and a Thomas Cook prize shortlisting – spawned a series that rapidly covered dozens of destinations. Rough Guides had a ready market among low budget backpackers, but soon also acquired a much broader and older readership that relished Rough Guides' wit and inquisitiveness as much as their enthusiastic, critical approach. Everyone wants value for money, but not at any price. Rough Guides soon began supplementing the "rougher" information about hostels and low-budget listings with the kind of detail on restaurants and quality hotels that independent-minded visitors on any budget might expect, whether on business in New York or trekking in Thailand. These days the guides offer recommendations from shoestring to luxury and they cover a large number of destinations around the globe, including almost every country in the Americas and Europe, more than half of Africa and most of Asia and Australasia. Rough Guides now publish:

- Travel guides to more than 200 worldwide destinations
- Dictionary phrasebooks to 22 major languages
- Maps printed on rip-proof and waterproof Polyart™ paper
- Music guides running the gamut from Opera to Elvis
- Reference books on topics as diverse as the Weather and Shakespeare
- World Music CDs in association with World Music Network

Visit **www.roughguides.com** to see our latest publications.

Publishing Information

This 1st edition published August 2004 by **Rough Guides Ltd**, 80 Strand, London WC2R 0RL. 345 Hudson St, 4th Floor, New York, NY 10014, USA.

Distributed by the Penguin Group
Penguin Books Ltd, 80 Strand, London WC2R 0RL
Penguin Group (USA), 375 Hudson Street, NY 10014, USA
Penguin Group (Australia), 487 Maroondah Highway, PO Box 257, Ringwood, Victoria 3134, Australia
Penguin Group (Canada), 10 Alcorn Avenue, Toronto, Ontario, Canada M4V 1E4
Penguin Group (NZ), 182–190 Wairau Road, Auckland 10, New Zealand
Typeset in Bembo and Helvetica to an original design by Henry Iles.
Printed and bound in Italy by Graphicom

160pp includes index
A catalogue record for this book is available from the British Library

ISBN 1-84353-321-9

The publishers and authors have done their best to ensure the accuracy and currency of all the information in **Marrakesh DIRECTIONS**, however, they can accept no responsibility for any loss, injury, or inconvenience sustained by any traveller as a result of information or advice contained in the guide.

1   3   5   7   9   8   6   4   2

Help us update

We've gone to a lot of effort to ensure that the first edition of **Marrakesh DIRECTIONS** is accurate and up-to-date. However, things change – places get "discovered", opening hours are notoriously fickle, restaurants and rooms raise prices or lower standards. If you feel we've got it wrong or left something out, we'd like to know, and if you can remember the address, the price, the phone number, so much the better.

We'll credit all contributions, and send a copy of the next edition (or any other DIRECTIONS guide or Rough Guide if you prefer) for the best letters. Everyone who writes to us and isn't already a subscriber will receive a copy of our full-colour thrice-yearly newsletter. Please mark letters: **"Marrakesh DIRECTIONS Update"** and send to: Rough Guides, 80 Strand, London WC2R 0RL, or Rough Guides, 4th Floor, 345 Hudson St, New York, NY 10014. Or send an email to **mail@roughguides.com**

Have your questions answered and tell others about your trip at **www.roughguides.atinfopop.com**

Rough Guide Credits

Text editor: Richard Lim
Layout: Andy Hilliard
Photography: Dan Eitzon
Cartography: Rajesh Chhibber, Animesh Pathak, Katie Lloyd-Jones, Ed Wright

Picture editor: Mark Thomas
Proofreader: Susannah Wight
Production: Julia Bovis
Design: Henry Iles
Cover art direction: Louise Boulton

The author

Daniel Jacobs is a major-league Moroccophile who has contributed to numerous Rough Guides, including the Morocco, Egypt, India, West Africa and Mexico titles. He is also the author of the *Rough Guide to Israel and the Palestinian Territories*, and co-author of the *Rough Guide to Tunisia*. He lives in south London.

Acknowledgements

From the author: Special thanks to Mark Ellingham for the use of text from the *Rough Guide to Morocco*. Many thanks also for help and advice in the making of this book to the Office National Marocain de Tourisme (ONMT) in Marrakesh and in London, and also to Don Grisbrook, Hamish Brown, James Stewart and James McConnachie. A special thank you to my editor, Richard Lim.

From the editor: Thanks to Andy Hilliard for layout, Mark Thomas for picture research; Rough Guides Delhi, Katie Lloyd-Jones and Ed Wright for cartography; and Susannah Wight for proofreading. Thanks also to Jamal Boujrad of the Moroccan National Tourist Office in London for advice and too many good coffees, and to Brahem of *Hotel La Gazelle* in Marrakesh for his hospitality.

Photo credits

All images © Rough Guides except the following:

Front cover picture: Orange stall © Corbis
Back cover picture: Koutoubia Mosque © Anthony Cassidy
Front cover flap: Gnaoua musician © Moroccan National Tourist Office
p.1 Marrakesh street signs © Travel Ink/Alamy
p.8 Essaouira ramparts © Hamish Brown
p.9 The Jemaa el Fna © Hamish Brown
p.9 Souk Smarine © Hamish Brown
p.10 Menara gardens © Moroccan National Tourist Office
p.13 Saadian Tombs © Hamish Brown
p.13 Majorelle Garden © Daniel Jacobs
p.18 Islamic Arts Museum © Daniel Jacobs
p.20 *La Mamounia* lobby courtesy of *La Mamounia Hotel*
p.23 Bâb Ighli © Daniel Jacobs
p.25 *Khondonjal* stall, Jemaa el Fna © Sandro Vannini/Corbis
p.40 Windsurfing at Essaouira © John Kirkpatrick/Alamy

p.41 Golf © Moroccan National Tourist Office
p.45 *Palais Gharnatta* courtesy of *Palais Gharnatta*
p.46 Moussem at Setti Fatma © Robert Harding Picture Library/Alamy
p.46 The Marrakesh Marathon courtesy of The Marrakesh Marathon
p.47 Marrakesh film festival © Stephane Cardinale/Corbis
p.47 Table set for Ramadan © Michelle Garrett/Corbis
p.48 Pavilion at the Menara gardens © Giraudou Laurent/Corbis Sygma
p.98 Atlas trekking © Hamish Brown
p.99 Essaouira © Hamish Brown
p.102 Boatyard in Essaouira © Hamish Brown
p.103 The Skala du Port, Essaouira © Daniel Jacobs
p.104 Essaouira from the Skala du Port © Daniel Jacobs
p.105 Seafood stall, Essaouira © Daniel Jacobs
p.106 Marine Gate, Essaouira © Daniel Jacobs

Index

Map entries are marked in colour

DIRECTIONS on Screen

Put the guide on your computer or PDA

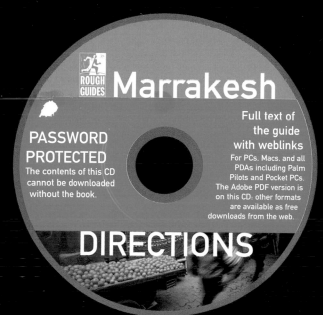

Marrakesh

PASSWORD PROTECTED
The contents of this CD cannot be downloaded without the book.

Full text of the guide with weblinks
For PCs, Macs, and all PDAs including Palm Pilots and Pocket PCs. The Adobe PDF version is on this CD; other formats are available as free downloads from the web.

DIRECTIONS

This CD contains the complete
Marrakesh DIRECTIONS
in Adobe PDF format, complete with maps and illustrations. PDFs are readable on any Windows or Mac-OS computer (including laptops). The mini-CD also contains instructions for further free downloads formatted for Pocket PC and Palm.

Insert the mini-CD in the central recess of any tray-loading CD-Rom drive: full instructions supplied. Note: mini-CDs will not work in slot-loading drives. Slot-loading drive owners or DIRECTIONS purchasers who have mislaid their mini-CD should go to www.directionsguides.com to download files as required. Note on platforms: Adobe supports maps and illustrations and is compatible with Mac and PC operating systems. Pocket PC and Palm platforms support text only.

www.roughguides.com

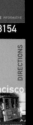